ELECTRONIC RESUMES FOR THE NEW JOB MARKET

ELECTRONIC RESUMES FOR THE NEW JOB MARKET

Peter D. Weddle

IMPACT PUBLICATIONS
Manassas Park, VA

ELECTRONIC RESUMES FOR
THE NEW JOB MARKET

Library of Congress Cataloguing-in-Publication Data

Weddle, Peter D.
    Electronic resumes for the new job market / Peter D. Weddle
      p. cm.
    Includes bibliographical references and index.
    ISBN 1-57023-008-0 : $11.95
    1. Resumés (Employment—Data processing. I. Title.
HF5383.W324 1994
808'.06665—dc20
                                              94-26613
                                                CIP

For information on distribution or quantity discount rates, Tel. 703/361-7300, Fax 703/335-9486, or write to: Sales Department, IMPACT PUBLICATIONS, 9104-N Manassas Drive, Manassas Park, VA 22111. Distributed to the trade by National Book Network, 4720 Boston Way, Suite A, Lanham, MD 20706, Tel. 301/459-8696.

For

John F. Joyce

comrade-in-arms and friend

ACKNOWLEDGMENTS

I am indebted to a large number of people for their generous assistance in writing this book. They include my good friends and professional colleagues, Joyce Lain Kennedy and Harvey Mackay; the staff of Job Bank USA, especially Andrew Vick, Shawn Thomas, Donna Fortney and Pam Monjar; Michael Losey, the President of the Society for Human Resource Management; my publishers, Ron and Caryl Krannich; and, of course, my family, especially Juliana, Meagan, Brooke and Peter. My thanks to you all for your counsel and support. Any errors or omissions which occur in the book are mine alone, however, and I take full responsibility for them.

CONTENTS

Section III: The Electronic Resume

Section IV: Write Your Electronic Resume Right

Job Bank Evaluation and Membership Resources

FORWARD

I like to watch the evening news when I get home from work each day. Usually that means that I miss the local newscast all together and have to content myself with the seven o'clock edition of the national news. So, each night I sit there on my sofa and listen to the stories that have been collected by the network to tell me about what's going on in the world.

Now, I know very little about international events, about health care issues, about crime, or poverty or any of the other issues and challenges we face in our hot tempered, end of the millennium society. I do, however, know something about the world of work and the state of employment in the United States. You see, I have the privilege of running a company called Job Bank USA and that puts me in a position to observe what's happening in the job market on a daily basis.

Job Bank USA is one of the leading electronic employment data base companies in the world. It recruits for some of the largest companies on earth and some of the smallest. It identifies candidates from our data base for open positions in virtually every occupational field, at all levels of experience and expertise, across all industries and in every region and country on the globe. For example, in the first quarter of 1993 alone, Job Bank USA recruited for open positions in all 48 contiguous states of the U.S. as well as in Latin America, Russia, the Middle East, and Africa. And every new quarter brings another whole array of employment opportunities located wherever our employer clients have sought to establish an operation.

I'll tell you more, later, about Job Bank USA and how you can use its unique capabilities to find the job you want and manage your career successfully in the 1990's. For the moment, however, I want to get back to the evening news, because its version of the employment situation in this country is **not** the same as mine.

To be sure, what is reported is accurate. The seemingly endless litany of corporate lay-offs, reductions-in-force, downsizings, rightsizings and restructuring actions by employers in the private sector and the government are painfully real for many Americans. Millions of jobs have been destroyed, and most economists and business experts expect this trend to continue through the end of the decade.

Today, millions of Americans are working at jobs beneath their skill levels because those are the only jobs they can get. Millions more are working in contingent positions that will end at some specified time in the future or in part-time positions because they cannot find a full time job. Millions more are working for themselves as "consultants" or "entrepreneurs," not because they want to, but because they have to. The results, as we see on the evening news each day, have touched almost all of us. Ourselves, our spouses, our kids, our relatives or our friends have all been affected by these huge changes in the American workplace.

All of this employment distress causes a level of anxiety and sense of diminished opportunity that is unprecedented in the United States since the Great Depression. Unfortunately, to the best of my knowledge, it's all true and correct. But more important, it is only half of the story!

New technology, new workplace designs, new management practices and just plain old fashioned growth are creating jobs at an historic pace. Contrary to popular notions, these are not positions flipping hamburgers. They are not dead end, low skill, minimum wage jobs. Indeed, many of these new positions hold far more challenge and opportunity than those which existed just five years ago, at the close of the Industrial Era. They are the stimulating, high skill, well paid jobs of the Electronic Era. And more positions just like them are being opened up every day.

An age of jobs built on strong backs, modest education and hierarchical organizations has ended. The Industrial Era in the U.S. has drawn to a close. In its place, a new age—the Electronic Era—is emerging. This new period is already creating millions of new jobs, but they are jobs that are very different from those that were produced by the manufacturing assembly line. Instead, these new jobs are the off spring of a tiny silicone wafer and integrated circuits, of complex and extraordinarily powerful technology that improves the quality and efficiency of work. As a result, the jobs that are being created today require in-depth training, state-of-the-art skills and re-designed processes and procedures. No less important, these Electronic Era positions collectively offer more interesting work, greater career advancement, and better compensation than any other jobs ever available to the general workforce

That's the other half of the story that you seldom hear about. And it creates an extraordinary choice for you. You can buy into the gloom and doom of the evening newscast and see the glass as half empty or you can acknowledge the difficulty of the current job market, but focus on its opportunity and see the glass as half full. I believe that the course you take will do much to determine the success or failure of your career.

See the glass half empty, and you've committed yourself to a career that is focused on survival and getting by. See the glass half full, and you will focus your career on a new frontier where there are virtually no limits to progress and moving ahead. The choice is yours, of course, but I encourage you to accept the latter outlook.

Why? Because I believe that the most accurate sign post for the world of work in the 1990's is:

"Don't Miss Out On the Opportunity!"

Whatever you do, don't get left behind.

There is much for you to accomplish and achieve in the workplace being created in the United States in the 1990's, **if** you'll just take advantage of it. It's a very different workplace than that of just five years ago, to be sure. All of that change we see on the evening news has had a profound impact on the job market and how you find, win and keep the job you want. In fact, the process has changed so completely and irrevocably, that I call it the New Job Market.

To succeed in this New Job Market, you're going to have to understand its ground rules and take advantage of new techniques and tools. The way you found a job and managed your career in the old job market of the Industrial Era won't do you much good in this new environment. Indeed, they can undermine and even hurt your prospects for success. So, I have written this book to introduce you to the New Job Market and to provide you with an exciting new tool to help you plumb its opportunities.

This new tool is an Electronic Resume. If I were going to use the latest management jargon to describe this document, I'd call it a "re-engineered" version of the conventional resume. Put more precisely, the Electronic Resume takes advantage of technology to expand and improve the impact of your resume. In essence, it is a resume that will work smart as well as work hard for you. Equally as important, it has been specifically designed to work and work well in the New Job Market.

Its purpose is to open the door for you at those organizations which have open positions for which you are qualified and in which you are interested. That's all an electronic resume or any resume, for that matter, can do. It won't "get" you a job. That's your role.

A well designed resume will attract the attention of an employer and get its representative to concentrate on your qualifications. That's no small feat in the New Job Market! Employers today are swamped with resumes from outstanding individuals who are seeking a new or better job. One report estimated that 1,000 unsolicited resumes a week arrive at most Fortune 500 companies, and 80% are tossed out after a quick review (*U.S. News & World Report*, October 26, 1992)! In such an environment, it's very difficult to set yourself apart from the crowd and get noticed. Hence, your resume has done its job, if it accomplishes that objective for you. Once an employer's door is open, it's up to you to convince the recruiter that you and your qualifications are the best for the job.

The Electronic Resume, therefore, is not a silver bullet. It won't help you win the lottery or lower your golf handicap. And it can't guarantee that you'll be offered the job of your dreams.

The Electronic Resume will, however, give you a genuine competitive advantage in the New Job Market. It will put the power of technology to work for you, so that more employers are aware of your occupational credentials. And, in the 1990's, those "electronic connections" are the keys to success in finding a new or better job. They enable you to vastly expand the number of employers who know about your skills and experience. In essence, the more people who know what you can do, the greater the likelihood that you will land one of those great new jobs being created in the Electronic Era. That's the power and the possibilities of the Electronic Resume.

This book will tell you how to write and distribute an Electronic Resume. The techniques are simple and easy to learn. Once you master them, you'll have a skill that few others can match, and that's a part of your edge. Combine that edge with the advantages provided by the Electronic Resume itself, and you've got a combination that will position you for success today, tomorrow and well into the next century!

Peter D. Weddle
McLean, Virginia

Section I

THE ELECTRONIC WORKPLACE

1

THE
ELECTRONIC
ERA

*T*wo startling changes occurred in the United States in 1991. Ironically, they received very little publicity or notice in the press. Yet, in many respects, they were watershed events, for they signaled this country's transition from an Industrial Era to a new social and economic age. I call this new period the Electronic Era. It's not a very catchy name, but it is accurate.

CHANGE AND REVOLUTION

In 1991, for the very first time, the cost of the microelectronics in your car exceeded the cost of the steel. On the average, you paid for $782 worth of electronic gadgetry and just $675 for the steel (*Fortune*, April 4, 1994). And that's just the beginning! From now on, when you purchase that quintessential expression of the American lifestyle—a car—you'll be spending more money on electronics in the engine and across the dashboard, than on anything else.

There's been a similar revolution underway in virtually every other aspect of

American living. American homes and recreation have been changed forever by the electronics in the television sets we watch, the microwave we use to cook our meals, the video games that captivate our kids (and some of us, as well), by our compact disc players, boom boxes, and the hand-held tape players we listen to while we jog. Electronics help us to communicate by cellular telephones and pagers and through hearing aids and by TDD devices. Electronics have created a new era in our country, and that period is indisputably shaping the lives of all of us through the convenience and pleasure provided by its products.

It should not be surprising, therefore, that electronics have begun to shape the world of work, as well. Indeed, in that same pivotal year of 1991, U.S. companies and corporations, for the very first time, spent more money on computers and telecommunications systems than they did on manufacturing, mining, construction and other equipment. As a consequence, the way American business works has been dramatically redefined and reshaped.

On the production line, robots now make more products to a higher standard of quality than we ever achieved in the Industrial Era. In retail companies, high speed management information systems are reducing the time and work required to identify customer preferences and deliver the most popular to store shelves. In service firms, the personal computer, the copier and the facsimile machine have reduced transaction times and improved flexibility, so that services can be customized to the specific needs of each client. As a result, electronics have helped make U.S. companies more competitive and increasingly successful in both our domestic economy and the global marketplace.

These changes, however, are not confined to the impersonal and distant arena of corporate strategy and economic competition. They have had an impact on each of us, as well. We shop in malls where we leave our cars in parking lots managed by electronic ticketing machines. We obtain our spending money from automatic teller machines and consult with electronic information kiosks that speed us on our way to just the store with the exact product for which we're looking. In that store, we are helped through our purchasing with electronic cash registers and bar code scanners, on-line credit card confirmation devices and door side security systems. Electronic devices make it all so easy and convenient that most of us have grown comfortable with their presence and dependent upon their benefits.

Indeed, the impact of the Electronic Era on our daily commerce is so pervasive as to be unremarkable. It's just there. The devices change from time-to-time, but mostly we've accepted that we live in an age when computer chips, miniaturized circuits and high speed processors will let us build things better, provide services more effectively and enjoy life more fully than ever before.

Unfortunately, however, it's not that simple. The Electronic Era has also begun to have a profound impact on our jobs and on the workplace and there, the changes are not so clearly beneficial.

The very same products of the Electronic Era that have made our homes and leisure pursuits so enjoyable and U.S. companies so competitive are dramatically reshaping the world of work. Processes and procedures, even the tasks and responsibilities of our jobs are changing significantly. As a consequence, the workplace and the job market of the 1990's are unlike any that you've ever seen before.

Part of this change is painful, as we know from the news each day. Computers and management information systems have eliminated tens of thousands of white collar, middle management jobs. Scanners, inventory control systems, and robots have cut just as many blue collar positions. These changes are permanent. They are not the result of a recession or a temporary economic downturn. Instead, they are the signs of a dramatic restructuring in the way we work. The resulting lay-offs, reductions-in-force, downsizings and restructurings have touched millions of Americans and left them uncertain about their security and opportunity in the future.

At the very same time, however, the electronic technology embedded in new devices and equipment is creating millions of new jobs. Contrary to popular notions, these are not dead end, "dummies only" jobs. In fact, many of these positions are high wage, high skill jobs offering great challenge and impressive rewards. To cite just two cases in point: In the past two years, Motorola has created 18,000 new jobs all by itself. Wal-Mart has done even better. In 1993 alone, Wal-Mart created 85,000 new jobs! Many of these positions at both companies are in the skilled technical trades, the white collar professions and management.

These new jobs, however, are part of a new kind of job market. It is a job market characterized by paradox, because it is simultaneously fraught with danger and virtually brimming with opportunity. It is as different from the job market of the 1980's as carbon paper is from copiers.

The New Job Market is a whole new ball game, and it operates with a totally new set of rules. The techniques for conducting a job search campaign today are completely different from those that worked and worked well just five years ago. Indeed, if you try to find a new or better job in the New Job Market using the old rules of job hunting, circa the 1980's, you'll expose yourself to considerable risk and deny yourself even more opportunity. Play the game using the new rules, however, and today's job market will create an almost unimaginable array of new possibilities to advance yourself in the world of work.

THE NEW JOB MARKET

I think the New Job Market is best described as "employment hyperspace." It is a jarring, fast-paced environment of job destruction and job creation, unlike any seen since the evolution of the U.S. from an agrarian to an industrial society. In the Industrial Era, for example, an organization's reputation was based on how big it was, and size was usually measured in numbers of employees. In the Electronic Era, on the other hand, global competition and shareholder demands have changed the metric of success. Today, an organization is regarded not by its size, but by its efficiency, a characteristic most often measured in terms of how much money it makes or how much value it provides. As a result, organizations have thrown themselves into crash diets that have shed millions of jobs. The sociology of today's corporation is heavily oriented toward flatter organizational structures with fewer employees at higher skill levels. Moreover, since competitive pressures continue unabated, there is every likelihood that these workforce reductions will continue throughout the 1990's.

Technological innovation is also redesigning organizations and jobs. Whole departments and divisions filled with labor intensive positions are being replaced with a smaller number of self-directed jobs with higher skill requirements. For example, manufacturing technology is destroying a growing number of positions that used to call for a person with a strong back and the basic reading, writing and arithmetic skills provided by a high school education. In their place, it is creating an array of new jobs that call for special skills in computer operation, electronic troubleshooting, systems analysis, and higher order computational skills. For those who have or acquire these skills, the prospect is for secure employment at higher levels of pay than were ever achieved in the old Industrial Era.

Further, this cycle of destruction and creation is not limited to blue collar jobs. Advanced information technology is fast destroying white collar middle management positions, as well. In their place are a growing number of positions that call for special skills in problem solving, group or team participation, and up-to-the-minute knowledge in specialized technical or professional fields. As with blue collar positions, these new white collar jobs offer incredible opportunity and reward for those who adjust and prepare themselves to perform capably.

These situations are not the product of a recession, but of a social and economic revolution. The changes they embody are permanent, widespread and seemingly random. More and more people today—people who have a job and work hard at it—are worried about being blindsided by the sale of their company, the closing of their plant, the introduction of a new machine that will replace them or a corporate strategy that will eliminate their job.

These changes, however, are not random. They are, instead, the leading edges of a new world of work and a New Job Market in the U.S. If you understand what's behind them and what they mean, you can manage them. You can be in charge of the changes in your career, rather than their victim.

Today's New Job Market has three very important characteristics which differentiate it from previous job markets:

- Warp speed jobs,
- High definition jobs, and
- Free agent employees.

Once you understand these unique differences, you'll have the foundation for successful job hunting and career management in the 1990's.

Warp Speed Jobs

In the Industrial Era, finding a good job was a challenge best described as "here today, gone tomorrow." You had to move quickly to find, win and keep the job you wanted. In the Electronic Era, however, the nature of your job search has changed dramatically. Today, finding a good job is best described as "here today, gone in nanoseconds."

The impact of electronics and other advances in technology have reduced the life cycle of a product to just 18 months. As a result, all of the jobs associated with each product—those in manufacturing, sales, marketing, distributing, even management—don't last much longer. What's that mean for you? Well, in the Industrial Era, you could probably count on changing jobs two, three, maybe even four times during your career. In the Electronic Era, however, it's more likely that you'll experience seven to ten job changes and perhaps as many as fifteen to twenty (U.S. Bureau of Labor Statistics). Indeed, you may even change careers three to five times! The only thing that's permanent about the New Job Market is change.

The symbol for career management in the Industrial Era was the gold watch. The idea was that you went to work for a single employer, spent virtually all of your career there and eventually retired from that organization. Your reward for all of those dedicated years of service was a gold watch and a good pension, if you were lucky.

In today's Electronic Era, on the other hand, the symbol for career management is not the gold watch, but the electronic remote control you use to change television channels. Today, tomorrow and into the next century, you will click rapidly through jobs, taking from each position the opportunity it presents to hone your skills and refine your capabilities in your chosen field of work and giving to each position and employer the benefit and value of that expanding competency. Although there will always be exceptions to the rule, it's now far more likely that you will change jobs and employers regularly and therefore retire from your profession, craft or trade, rather than from a career spent with just one organization.

High Definition Jobs

As technology roars into all corners of the workplace, the specific skills required for job performance become more exact and specific. The pace of technological development has become so rapid that 50% of your skills grow obsolete every three to five years ("Human Resource Measurements," Wonderlic Personnel Test, Inc.). That means, of course, that you must view yourself as a work-in-progress. Your education and training are never done in the Electronic Era. Instead, you will always be involved in acquiring new skills for the job you have today and for the new job you will inevitably have in the future.

These new skills are essential to high caliber job performance. Today your co-worker on the job is, more often than not, a technologically advanced system or piece of equipment. To do your part and meet your responsibilities, you have to know how to interact with that technology and work with it on-the-job. As each piece of equipment and technology requires a specific set of skills, employers are becoming increasingly detailed about the array of capabilities and experiences that a person must have to be considered qualified for an open position.

In fact, this specialization of competencies has changed the basic nature of recruiting. In the Industrial Era, when many jobs were similar and technology was much less intrusive in the design of jobs, the rule of thumb for successful recruiting was to "get the round peg in the round hole." Although not everyone could fit into every job (square pegs just didn't fit into round holes), the basic premise was that all round pegs were alike and so were all round jobs. In essence, people were interchangeable to a great degree.

In the Electronic Era, however, recruiting takes a fundamentally different approach. Now, many jobs are so different and unique, that recruiting for them is like opening a lock. Employers believe that only a very special person with a very specific set of qualifications can be the right person to open the lock. No less important, they are willing to wait until they find just that person—the single person with the precise set of skills they want—to fill their open position. Hence, the more specialized and more up-to-date your occupational credentials, the higher the probability that you will be competitive for the jobs being created in the New Job Market.

Free Agent Employees

In the Industrial Era, you could count on your employer to manage your career for you. Particularly if you worked for a big company, you knew that the organization would (a) place you in a career path that defined your opportunity in the organization, (b) select and assign you to those jobs that would optimize your contribution to the organization, (c) ensure that you were trained for the jobs you held and (d) move you along your career path to the appropriate level for your maximum contribution and level of performance. All you had to do was be loyal and work hard. Everything else was taken care of.

It was a very paternalistic system, and although there was precious little room for individuality and flexibility, many people found it to be a comfortable and reasonably secure arrangement. In the Electronic Era, however, companies have neither the resources nor the inclination to continue playing such a role. The competition is too tough and budgets are too tight for organizations to be able to manage the careers of their employees. Instead, in the Electronic Era, everyone is on their own. We've gone from being "employer-reliant" to being "self-reliant."

As a result, from now on, you will have two jobs in the world of work: (1) to be a state-of-the-art performer in the high definition jobs you want in your chosen occupational field and (2) to manage your own career so that you have the qualifications you need to protect yourself from and compete for the warp speed jobs in the New Job Market. That means it's **your** job to select the positions that will provide you with the greatest challenge and opportunity; it's **your** job to get the skills and experience to compete for those positions; it's **your** job to find out where those positions are located; and it's **your** job to make sure that the employers which have those positions know you and your credentials. In essence, you're a free agent **and** the manager of your own career.

A WORLD OF NEW OPPORTUNITIES

The Electronic Era is producing monumental change in the way we live our lives and in the way we work. It is altering the nature of the jobs we hold and creating a New Job Market. This "employment hyperspace" can look and feel like chaos, but it's not. Instead, the New Job Market is the explosive creation of opportunity. The Electronic Era is destroying millions of Industrial Era jobs and simultaneously replacing them with millions of new positions. Hence, it holds both great danger and extraordinary rewards.

That's the challenge you face in the New Job Market. Fail to recognize and adjust to those changes and you will seriously hurt your ability to find, win and keep the jobs you want in the years ahead. If you accept these changes, however, and learn about them and prepare to work with them, you will acquire a huge competitive advantage in the job market. You'll be playing the game as it actually exists, with the rules as they actually are, and that will inevitably put you ahead of the pack.

The New Job Market requires a whole array of new skills for managing your career and for conducting a job search successfully. How do you survive and prosper in such an environment? The chapter which follows will discuss these new skills.

2

HOW TO SURVIVE AND PROSPER IN THE NEW JOB MARKET

*T*here are several rules for success in the New Job Market. At first, these rules may seem strange and even feel uncomfortable to you. That's because they are new and different, not because they are wrong. These new rules were designed for today's and tomorrow's job market; they are unlike anything you may have learned about finding a job in the old Industrial Era. And that's entirely appropriate because, by-and-large, that old job market is gone forever.

NEW RULES AND BENEFITS

The rules for surviving and prospering in the dynamic New Job Market are:

1. Keep your credentials in constant circulation;
2. Distribute your credentials as broadly as possible;
3. Practice perpetual documentation with your resume;

9

4. Exercise total control over your job search; and

5. Lead with your strengths by building Career Fitness.

Each of these rules is described below. If you follow them, you'll gain two advantages. First, they will help you plug into the employment hyperspace of the 1990's. Second, they will connect you with the job opportunities that are being created at warp speed in the New Job Market. As a result, you will

1. Dramatically increase the number and quality of jobs available to you and

2. Ensure that you are seriously considered for those you would most like to have.

The benefits of those two advantages are especially important to you. First, they will create a safety net of continuous employment opportunity. You'll be under constant consideration for great job openings just in case your current job disappears, for whatever reason. Indeed, as you will shortly see, this approach enables you to be more proactive, to anticipate threats to your current employment and to do something about them even while you are still at work on-the-job. In effect, your job search doesn't begin from a standing start, with all of the delays and frustrations that involves. Instead, your job search is always underway, in high gear, so that you are already well on your way to finding a new job while others are still getting organized and figuring out what to do. Like a "career insurance" policy, this approach ensures that opportunity is there if and when you need it.

Second, being plugged into employment hyperspace is a way to further the advancement of your career. Unfortunately, the movement to flatter organizations among U.S. companies has significantly diminished the opportunity for upward mobility. Hence, in many cases today, the only way to advance your career is to seek a new position in a different organization. If opportunity still exists in your current employer's organization, that's great. Take advantage of it. But if there is no room for you to improve yourself and to advance your level of expertise and experience with your current employer, then it is **your** responsibility as your own career manager to look elsewhere. And, the best way to do that is to plug into the New Job Market and connect with its employment opportunities.

RULE ONE: KEEP YOUR RESUME IN CONSTANT CIRCULATION

The first requirement for success in the New Job Market is to keep your resume in constant circulation when you're employed and when you're not. You must always have your resume out there among prospective employers, so that they know who you are and what qualifications you can offer them on-the-job.

In the Industrial Era, it was considered disloyal to put your resume into the job market while you were still working for an employer. In the New Job Market, however, the definition of loyalty has expanded. Now you must be loyal to your employer **and** loyal to yourself. The loyalty that you owe to your employer is to deliver the best performance you can on-the-job, not to remain employed in that job forever. The loyalty that you owe to yourself and to your family is to protect your ability to work. Indeed, in today's New Job Market, loyalty to yourself is a matter of survival. You need a safety net to protect you from job changes initiated by your employer, and you need to find new career opportunities for yourself. Moreover, most career counselors have long agreed that the best time to find a new job is while you are employed, not when you're out of work. And the only way to do that, of course, is to keep your work credentials in circulation all of the time.

So, in the New Job Market, you have to find a way to keep your resume in circulation while you are still at work in your current position. You also have to get beyond the limitations of your own time and energy and keep your resume in circulation while you are on vacation, running errands, even while you're asleep. In other words, constant circulation means putting your resume into play 24 hours a day, 7 days a week, 365 days a year. Resume circulation is a full time process that must never stop.

RULE TWO: DISTRIBUTE YOUR CREDENTIALS AS BROADLY AS POSSIBLE

The best way to keep your resume in circulation is to broadcast it as widely as possible. Even if you think that you will never move outside your current community or take a job in an industry other than the one in which you now work, it's critical that you not limit the range of your resume's distribution. In the New Job Market, exciting new opportunities can appear anywhere, any time. The only way to ensure that you will even know about them is to keep your resume circulating as widely as possible. You can always turn a position down if you decide it's not right for you, but you'll never have that chance (or, more importantly, the chance to *accept* that job), if the employer simply hasn't heard of you. So, the best rule of thumb for circulating your resume in the 1990's is to impose absolutely no limits. The further afield the better.

Of course, that means you should continue to do all of the things that you have traditionally done to get your resume into circulation:

- Answer recruitment ads in newspapers,
- Use the telephone to prospect for job openings with employers,
- Contact headhunters and other recruiters who specialize in your field, and
- Network among your friends and colleagues.

In the New Job Market, however, doing all of that is important, but it's no longer enough. Too many other job seekers are in the market doing the same thing. Hence, you have to do something else to increase the range of your resume and to put it into niches of the job market with which you are not personally familiar. Your goal is to connect with what's called "the hidden job market."

The hidden job market is the vast number of employment positions which are never advertised and hence remain unknown to most people. Ironically, these are some the best available opportunities. They are often great jobs that are almost always filled without a lot of public fanfare or visibility. One of the keys to success in the New Job Market, therefore, is to ensure that your resume gets considered for as many of these hidden jobs as possible.

RULE THREE: PRACTICE PERPETUAL DOCUMENTATION WITH YOUR RESUME

In the old job market of the Industrial Era, most people didn't expect to change jobs with any degree of frequency, so they seldom prepared themselves in advance for a job search. That usually meant that you didn't "do your resume" until you were actually out of work and in the job market. At that point, however, developing a resume becomes a monumental effort under great pressure. Job opportunities are being lost while you slog your way through (1) learning the skills required for writing a good resume, (2) making decisions about your job search objective, (3) identifying the appropriate skills and experience you should document on your resume in support of your objective, and (4) creating a final document that will work effectively for you in the job market. The whole process slowed down the pace of your job search and could even critically undermine its success.

An out-of-date resume was harmful enough in the Industrial Era job market, but in the New Job Market, it can be fatal. Since success in the New Job Market requires that you keep your resume in constant circulation, you must always have such a document ready, and it must always be up-to-date. Indeed, from now on, your resume must be "a living document." It must be complete and accurate. And, it must record changes in your skills, abilities, and experience at the moment they occur.

There's no other way to compete for the jobs you want in the New Job Market. Jobs come and go too fast. An out-of-date resume simply will not represent you well in the fierce competition for the great jobs in today's employment hyperspace. In fact, I believe it signals a level of personal carelessness and irresponsibility from which any employer will shy away. So, to make sure you aren't overlooked or under-evaluated for the employment opportunities of the 1990's, you must always have a complete and up-to-date resume in circulation.

RULE FOUR: EXERCISE TOTAL CONTROL OVER YOUR JOB SEARCH

In the Industrial Era job market, job seekers were warned always to keep control over the distribution of their resume. You were cautioned to know where your resume was being sent and for what opportunity, particularly if you were looking for a new job while still working for another employer. Total control was the only way that you could ensure the confidentiality of your job search, and that confidentiality was the best way you could protect yourself from an embarrassing and potentially dangerous situation with your current employer.

The same is true of the New Job Market. Confidentiality has the same virtue and benefits. Indeed, it may be even more important today. That's because you want to keep your resume in circulation broadly in order to stay abreast of the opportunities being created in the job market. The success of that strategy, however, depends, in part, on your ability to broadcast your resume as widely as possible without having to worry about it landing on your boss's desk.

In addition, you want to be sure that you are considered only for the jobs that are of interest to you. Total control over the circulation of your resume prevents you from being hurt because you were considered for the wrong job. Nothing upsets a prospective employer more than to spend the time and energy involved in considering a candidate seriously for an open job, only to discover later that he/she has no interest in it. When that situation occurs, it makes the candidate look unprofessional and even inconsiderate—not the kind of reputation that will stand you in good stead in subsequent job searches.

Consequently, any loss of control in the job market can hurt you badly. You cannot take too many precautions to ensure that your job search is private and that **you** determine where and when you will be considered for an open position. On the other hand, keeping proactive control, when coupled with constant, broadcast distribution of your resume, can pay handsome dividends in the number and quality of opportunities for which you are considered in the New Job Market.

RULE FIVE: LEAD WITH YOUR STRENGTHS BY BUILDING CAREER FITNESS

The first four rules above are key principles that will help you connect with the employment opportunities being created every day in the New Job Market. They will not, however, ensure that you capture those opportunities; they will not, by themselves, enable you to win the jobs you want.

You can put your resume in circulation all of the time; you can broadcast it widely in the job market; and you can keep your resume up-to-date and remain in total control of your job search and still come away empty handed. Why? Because your appeal to prospective employees is based on the strength of your occupational skills, not your talent for distributing your resume. If your resume describes a brain dead worker, you can circulate it as broadly as you like, but it won't do you any good. You won't be of interest to any of the employers with open positions to fill.

Career Fitness is a philosophy of working and a set of practical, everyday exercises that will help you identify and build your occupational strengths. As with physical fitness, improving your Career Fitness is something only you can do for yourself, and you must work on every day. It's your job to manage your career, and it's a job that's just as important as the one you do for your employer. Indeed, a healthy career is the best way to build job security for yourself and to enhance the paycheck and the satisfaction you bring home from work each day. And that's the purpose of Career Fitness.

There are a number of techniques and an array of steps involved in developing Career Fitness. They are all designed, however, to help you achieve a single, critical goal: to enable you to Be Your Personal Best in the field of work you most enjoy. To do so, you must keep your skills at the state-of-the-art in your occupation and acquire new capabilities—valued added skills in oral and written communications and foreign languages; in financial management and other aspects of running a business; in computer literacy, word processing and spreadsheet analysis; and in teamwork and leadership, particularly among a diverse workforce organized and operating in teams—that will improve the impact of your work. (For a complete introduction to Career Fitness, please see my book, *Career Fitness*, Cadell & Davies, 1994.) When you have these kinds of occupational strengths **and** you document them in your resume, circulate them broadly and constantly in the job market but control where they go and when, you'll have an enormous advantage in finding, winning and keeping the jobs you want in the 1990's.

The next sections of the book will tell you how you can put these rules to work. Chapter 3 will introduce you to a technique for plugging into the employment hyperspace of the New Job Market, while Chapter 4 will show you how to put that technique to work broadcasting your credentials effectively to the right employers with the right jobs for you at the right time.

Section II

THE NEW JOB MARKET

3

ELECTRONIC NETWORKING IN THE NEW JOB MARKET

*T*he conventional wisdom in the Industrial Era job market was simple: the best way to find a good job was through networking. That principle recognized the fact that most open positions are not advertised. They were a part of that "hidden job market." To uncover these positions, you had to talk to people who knew about them or who knew the hiring managers in the organizations where they were located. Those contacts, in turn, enabled you to get your credentials into the competition. They would help you find the opportunities available in the "hidden job market." Hence, the more people you contacted, the more networking you did, the better the odds that you would find the right position for you.

DISCOVER A NEW WORLD OF NETWORKING

In the Industrial Era, the way you networked was to steadily increase the number of people whom you knew. You were searching for just the right person who could then connect you with the best available position for you. Hence, the more people **you** knew the better the odds of finding that special job.

In the Electronic Era, however, networking is different. Given the dynamics of the New Job Market, the best way to network now is not to increase the number of people whom **you** know, but rather to increase the number of people who know you. The more people who are aware of your credentials and qualifications, the higher the probability that you will be considered for an employment opportunity. The key to successful networking in the New Job Market, therefore, is to find a way to increase the range and visibility of your resume.

And that's the rub. Conventional networking is limited to the number of people you can contact at any given time. It's very labor intensive and depends entirely on you. The more time and effort you spend, the greater the number of contacts you have. Unfortunately, you and all of us only have so much time to spend. We have other things going on in our lives. We need to eat from time-to-time. We need to sleep, go to work, spend time with our families and friends. While some limited networking can occur while we're doing those things, in most cases, we have limited time available to work our contacts.

Success in the New Job Market, therefore, is dependent upon your finding a way to overcome the limitations imposed on your own time, so that you can increase the number of people who know about you. Fortunately, the same electronics that have imposed so many changes on our lifestyles and our workplace have also made possible a solution to this dilemma. This solution captures the power and speed of advanced technology and harnesses it to the task of broadcasting your credentials throughout the "hidden job market." It's the difference between tramping by foot through the job market and moving at the speed of light by using electronic technology. Hence, I call this technique "electronic networking."

Electronic networking is a way to augment the networking you can and should do on your own. It is not a substitute for conventional networking, responding to classified ads or any of the other traditional strategies for finding a job. Instead, it is a new and powerful technique that you can **add** to these tried and true techniques to improve the effectiveness and success of your job search.

Electronic networking puts your resume into circulation through a computer.

The computer then matches your work credentials with the requirements specified for open jobs and connects you with the appropriate employer. It's still up to you to land the job, but the computer has opened the door for you and "made the introduction." Hence, electronic networking provides the same benefit as conventional networking; it puts you in touch with more of the employment opportunities in the "hidden job market."

LEARN TO "SEE"

Electronic networking, however, has an additional advantage. It enables you to **SEE**. If it's done correctly, electronic networking gives you visibility in the job market and access to employment opportunities in a way that is **S**afe, **E**ffective and **E**fficient.

Safe: Electronic networking is safe because you can control what happens to your resume after the computer makes a match for you. The computer does all of the work, but you're still in charge.

Effective: Electronic networking is also effective because it expands the range of positions you can contact beyond those available to you in the classified ads and through your own conventional networking. In addition, it can connect you with the vast array of unadvertised employment opportunities in the "hidden job market."

Efficient: Electronic networking is efficient because that computer never has to sleep, eat or take a rest. Hence, it works on your behalf 24 hours a day, 7 days a week, 365 days a year. Electronic networking puts your credentials into circulation while you're on another job interview, while you're at work in your current job, even while you're on vacation or taking a nap on the sofa!

ACQUIRE A SPECIAL EDGE

Electronic networking also gives you a special edge. Experts in networking have always instructed job seekers that the term "network" means net **work**, *not* net **play** or net **relax**. In other words, networking is helpful only when you make it an integral part of your work day and only when you do it regularly. It's a sound and very important principle for the traditional networking that you do for yourself.

With electronic networking, however, you expand the range of your connections and off load the work involved to the computer. In effect, electronic networking puts the power of advanced technology to work for you. It enables you to work smart as well as work hard. No less important, it creates a new kind of distribution system for your resume that will plug you into the New Job Market.

Electronic networking doesn't happen all by itself, however. It's a capability that you can obtain only through an electronic employment data base company, an electronic job bank or just a "job bank" for short. The next chapter will describe how a job bank works and what you can expect from the electronic networking it will do on your behalf.

4

ELECTRONIC JOB BANKS FOR PLUGGING INTO THE NEW JOB MARKET

*E*lectronic networking is possible today because of the widespread growth of electronic employment data base companies. I call these companies electronic job banks or just "job banks," for short. A job bank builds a data base containing the resumes of prospective employees in one or more fields and sells access to that data base to employers with open positions.

JOB BANK RESOURCES

Most job banks are operated by for-profit companies, although there are a number of similar services provided by associations and alumni organizations for their members. Commercial job banks vary widely in their size and scope of operation. Some may focus on a certain segment of the workforce (e.g., HispanData is a data base for Hispanic college graduates). Others will concentrate on a specific occupational field (e.g., the American Society of

Association Executives has a data base for people seeking career positions in the management of not-for-profit organizations). Still others operate data bases that cover the full range of occupational fields and industries (e.g., Job Bank USA covers all professions, crafts, and trades, at all management and skill levels, across all industries, nationwide).

Whether the job bank is operated by a for-profit company or by an association or alumni organization, most charge a fee for their service. Employers pay a fee to access the candidates in the data base for their open positions. These fees range from several hundreds to several thousands of dollars per single use of the data base. Individuals, on the other hand, pay a much smaller fee to enroll their employment credentials in the data base for a specified period of time. These fees range from a nominal sum of $25.00 or less to several hundreds of dollars.

There are many variations in the services provided by job banks. Some job banks focus on helping people who are already in the job market and actively conducting a job search. They view their service as a short term additional resource you can use to find new employment opportunities. As a result, you are required to re-enroll your credentials every three months or so, to stay active in their data base.

Other job banks view their service as a way for individuals to "troll" for new or better jobs. The focus is not on finding a position in the short term, but on keeping your credentials in circulation over the mid to long term, to see what comes along. Normally, you are required to re-enroll on an annual basis for such job banks.

A third kind of job bank—including Job Bank USA—sees itself as all of the above **and** a resource for acquiring the skills, knowledge and tools required for a successful job search in the 1990's. That means the job bank provides all of the advantages of electronic networking **plus** access to information, books and services to improve your skills in prospecting for jobs, interviewing, and negotiating your salary. With the New Job Market characterized by free agency, this kind of job bank can help you both find a new or better job and manage your career effectively.

FUNCTIONS AND SERVICES

Whatever their focus, however, all job banks use computer-based technology to match the right people with the right skills to the right employer with the right jobs. Here's how they work.

First, the employment company purchases or leases a computer and purchases or develops a software program which can store and manage a data base. Early job banks were built on main frame computers because employment information usually involves a significant amount of text, requiring a large data base for storage. Technological advances in computers, however, enable many of today's job banks to run on personal computers linked together in a network. Whatever the hardware and software used by the company, the computer must be able to (a) store resumes or other employment related information in a data base, (b) search among all of the resumes/employment information in the data base and identify those files that meet the specific criteria for a position vacancy, (c) print out the information contained in the specified resumes/files to forward it to employers, and (d) then return the resume/files to the data base for future use.

Second, the company fills the data base with resumes or other employment information obtained from individuals seeking new or different jobs. There are several ways this information is collected: (a) enrollment forms, on which the individual is asked to provide either an employment summary or profile, or a complete work history; (b) the individual's resume; and (c) a combination of an enrollment form and resume. In the 1960's and 1970's, this information was normally entered into the data base by typing it into the computer. Today, many of the job banks use a new technology called "optical character recognition" software and special devices to scan the information into the data base. This technology "takes a picture" of a person's resume and then translates that image into data which a computer can recognize and store.

Third, the company offers access to the data base to employers as a way to find and select employment candidates for their open positions. Some job banks permit the employer to link up to their computer and search the data base directly. Other job banks collect the necessary information about the open position and then search the data base for the employer. In either case, the employer receives information about prospective candidates whose qualifications match some or all of the requirements established for an open job. As with a classified ad in a newspaper, it is then up to the employer to evaluate this information and decide which of the candidates will be contacted.

More and more employers are turning to job banks to supplement their traditional recruiting strategies because they provide a number of important advantages:

- **Workload reduction.** The computer eliminates the need for the employer's staff to sort through and evaluate stacks of paper resumes.

- **Speed.** The computer works faster than human staff to evaluate employment credentials and identify qualified candidates.

- **Accuracy.** The computer doesn't overlook or miss key data in a candidate's record and hence ensures that all qualified individuals will be identified.

Today, recruiters and hiring managers expect the same efficiency and productivity in their recruiting activities as they do in their other operations. The use of job banks is spreading rapidly among employers of all sizes because job banks capture the power and accuracy of computers and put them to work matching individuals with the right skills to employers with the right jobs, at the right time.

WHAT DOES A JOB BANK DO FOR YOU?

As we've already noted, the Electronic Era is creating a vast number of challenging and rewarding new jobs, while simultaneously destroying millions of obsolete Industrial Era positions. The resulting New Job Market is a hyperspace of fast-moving employment opportunities and extraordinary new career options. In order to tap its potential for your career, you need a way to plug into the employment hyperspace. And that's precisely what a job bank will do. It uses the efficiency and effectiveness of advanced computer technology to put your employment credentials into circulation broadly so that you are considered for a large number of employment opportunities the moment they appear in the New Job Market. In short, a job bank is an "opportunity finder."

Responding to classified ads, telephone prospecting and other traditional job search activities will also put your credentials into circulation. You should continue to do all of these things, but now you can add the advantages of a job bank to your job search arsenal. These advantages are significant and unique to the technology a job bank puts to work on your behalf.

The most important, of course, is "electronic networking." That computer doesn't need to sleep or take a vacation. It operates continuously to connect you with employment opportunities that you wouldn't otherwise even know are available. In essence, a job bank enables you to expand your job search by increasing the time you have available for networking and the range of contacts you can make. While others may be networking a couple of hours a day among their friends and colleagues, electronic networking connects you with prospective employers well beyond your personal circle of contacts and does so 24 hours a day, 7 days a week, 365 days a year. As a result, it increases the number of people who know **you**.

In addition, a job bank helps to protect you from unethical or illegal treatment by creating an "electronic level playing field." The job bank's computer has no prejudices or biases. It doesn't care about your gender, ethnicity, age, or disabilities. Hence, everyone has a fair and equal shot at each open job. For the computer, the sole criterion for selection is the match between a person's skills and experience and the qualifications specified for successful job performance. Although it's possible to manipulate a computer to search for inappropriate attributes, most job banks scrupulously protect the integrity of their searches by focusing their computers exclusively on job performance criteria. At Job Bank USA, for example, we don't even collect gender, ethnicity, disability or age data. Hence, the **only** match our computer can make is between the skills people have and the skills jobs require.

Finally, a job bank can actually expand the hours in your day and the days in your week. It gives you the flexibility to be doing other things, while you're looking for a new or better job. In effect, a job bank can be your own personal "electronic career assistant," which will work the job market for you, so that you can spend time with your family or continue to work at your current job.

YOUR NEW OPPORTUNITY FINDER

Job banks are not a panacea, however. Unfortunately, they cannot "get" you a job. In fact, no employment service, consultant or agency can do that for you. The truth is that only **you** can get you a job. A job bank will plug you into the jobs its client employers have asked it to fill. As these are high definition jobs with very specific skill requirements, there can be no guarantee that you will qualify for any of these positions. On the other hand, you do have every right to expect the job bank **to guarantee** that you will be fully and fairly considered for each and every one of those opportunities.

Further, as we have discussed, the key to a successful job search in the New Job Market is to increase the number of employers who are aware of your credentials. A job bank is an innovative, new resource to help you do that, in a timely and cost effective way. No one resource, however, can give you access to all of the opportunities that are available. Therefore, you should integrate your use of a job bank into a comprehensive job search strategy which includes networking, responding to recruitment ads, and all of the other components of a conventional job search.

At the bottom line, a job bank is an opportunity finder and a personal referral service in the employment hyperspace of the New Job Market. It's a powerful new resource that can give you a genuine competitive advantage in your quest for the best available jobs for you. But, how do you know which job bank to use? There are hundreds, maybe thousands of job banks out there, and it's very difficult to differentiate one from another. The next chapter will tell you how to evaluate all of these job banks and how to select the one that will work best for you.

5

HOW TO PICK THE RIGHT JOB BANK

*D*espite their potential benefits, job banks have had a checkered record, over the past thirty years. There have been a number of serious flaws in the way job banks have delivered their services which have, in turn, diminished their value to individuals and employers alike. Although many of today's job banks have made significant improvements in their capabilities and performance, you should exercise considerable care in picking a job bank to work for you. To help you with your evaluation, let's review some of the problems which job banks have experienced in the past.

PROBLEMS AND PROMISES

Since their inception in the 1960's, job banks have had a fascination for both individual job seekers and for employers seeking access to high caliber employment candidates. Until recently, however, employers have been slow to

29

use them because the quality of the information they provided was often poor. Many of the early job banks did not keep their records up-to-date, so the information in their data base did not help prospective employers. There were instances when employers received resumes or employment files on individuals who had relocated and were not interested in the open position. In other cases, the files provided were for individuals who had left the job market or found another job. There were even stories of employers receiving referrals for individuals who had died.

Compounding this poor record of quality assurance were operating procedures that made job banks difficult to use and expensive. Many of the early job banks required the employer to access the data base by computer. In other words, the employer had to be "on-line" with the job bank in order to use it. That meant that the recruiter had to have a computer, a modem, the right software and the skills and knowledge to use the system effectively. Further, the employer was often charged one fee to enter the data base, another fee for the time spent searching the data base and yet a third fee for printed copies of the employment records of those individuals identified as qualified candidates for an open position.

What's all this have to do with you? Well, if employers found job banks too much trouble to use, then job banks had precious few employment opportunities to offer to the individuals enrolled in the data base. Indeed, they were not **job banks** at all. Instead, they were great big, useless data bases of resumes. That was, unfortunately, all too often the case in the past.

Today, however, most job banks have instituted some sort of process for reviewing and updating the information in their data bases. Although these quality control procedures vary widely from job bank to job bank, they have, in many cases, dramatically improved the accuracy and usefulness of the information provided by job banks. Hence, more and more employers are trying them out to see how they work and what they can do.

Individuals have also had their problems with job banks. Some of these services have been established by companies which lack the financial resources or the recruiting skills necessary to build a successful operation. Others have been too small or too narrowly focused in terms of the candidates in their data bases to convince employers to use them. As a result, they have had few employment opportunities to offer to their participants. Whatever the cause, many of these job banks failed, leaving those who enrolled in the dark about what happened to their records and at a loss for the money they paid to participate.

Selecting a job bank, therefore, is a critical and sometimes difficult decision.

A good job bank can provide you with all of the benefits of electronic networking and more. It can plug you into the employment hyperspace of the New Job Market. And it can match you with an array of exciting job opportunities. The wrong job bank, on the other hand, is a waste of your time and your money.

The questionnaire which follows, therefore, has been designed to help you to evaluate job banks, so that you can select the best one for you. It is not a scientific survey, but a structured interview which will identify key information about different job banks, so that you can make a logical and meaningful comparison. For a relatively complete listing of the available job banks in the U.S., see Joyce Lain Kennedy and Thomas J. Morrow's book, *Electronic Job Search Revolution* (John Wiley & Sons, 1994).

THE JOB BANK EVALUATION QUESTIONNAIRE

The following questionnaire compiles information on ten different aspects of a job bank's operations and reputation. Appendix A provides a worksheet for compiling the answers to the questions for each of the different job banks you consider. The answers to the questions for Job Bank USA have already been entered in the worksheet.

1. **How long has the job bank been in business?** If the job bank has been in operation for less than a year, you're taking a risk to use it.

2. **How many employers use the job bank to recruit?** If the job bank won't tell you how many employer clients it has and/or won't give you some or all of the names of those clients for which it has worked in the past twelve months, you're taking a risk to use it.

3. **How many searches did the job bank do in the past twelve months?** The bigger the number the better. The key, however, is the ratio of job searches to individuals enrolled in the data base. If the ratio is more than twenty-five (25) individuals per search, you're not likely to get much out of your experience.

4. **How many people are in the job bank's data base?** If the job bank has fewer than 10,000 resumes or employment records in its data base, it's unlikely that employers will find it much use for their recruiting

assignments. If employers don't use the data base, it's providing little in the way of employment opportunity for you.

5. **How many people in the data base were actually matched for an employment opportunity in the past year?** If the job bank matches fewer than 25% of the people in its data base annually, then its value to you is diminished. This situation usually occurs because the job bank doesn't have a large volume of on-going searches for employers or because it uses weak search software, making it difficult to identify qualified people in the data base.

6. **How many people in the data base were interviewed by the employers to which they were referred in the past year?** A job bank has done its job when it matches a qualified candidate with an employer's open position. However, if less than 50% of the referred candidates go on to get interviews with the employer, than the quality of that match is suspect and its value to you is diminished.

7. **Does the job bank let you modify or update your resume?** If you can't or the job bank charges you a fee to do so, it's likely that the quality of the information contained in the data base is poor. Employers will quickly identify this problem and simply take their business (and your employment opportunities) to another job bank.

8. **What information does the job bank provide about you to employers?** If the job bank provides a look-alike, computer-generated profile or summary of occupational credentials for everyone it refers, you'll lose some of the key features that will help to differentiate you from the competition. Most recruiters prefer that a job bank forward a copy of your original paper-based resume because the "look and feel" of that document tells them a great deal about you, the individual.

9. **What safeguards does the job bank use to protect your confidentiality?** Most job banks allow you to "block" your resume from being sent to one or more employers, including of course, the organization for which you are currently working. A smaller number of job banks use a safer system involving direct contact with the individual to obtain his/her approval before a resume is released to a prospective employer.

10. **What organizations, associations, societies and other groups endorse the job bank?** A track record is the best evidence that a job bank will perform as advertised. And the best track record is one composed of testimonials by organizations which have used the service. If the job bank can't provide these testimonials, you're taking a risk to use it.

The above questionnaire isn't fail safe, but it will give you the information you need to make a careful assessment of the different job banks in the marketplace. Virtually anyone with a personal computer can set themselves up in the job bank business, so such care is both appropriate and prudent. Moreover, the effort is especially worthwhile because a good job bank can plug you into a whole new spectrum of employment opportunities and, through the efficiency and effectiveness of its technology, ensure that you are fairly and fully evaluated for each and every one of them.

To put yourself in the best possible position for that evaluation and to give yourself the best chance of actually connecting with one or more available positions, you need a new kind of employment record. I call this record an "electronic resume," because it is specifically designed to be read and evaluated by a computer-based job bank. The next section will introduce you to the power and capabilities of the electronic resume and describe its key elements in detail.

Section III

THE ELECTRONIC RESUME

6

THE POWER OF ELECTRONIC RESUMES

*A*n electronic resume is similar to a conventional resume in that it is a record of your occupational credentials and experience. An electronic resume, however, is specifically designed, to be read by a computer. Such a design is critically important because it best positions you to connect with the employment opportunities available in a job bank. In other words, the job bank will plug you into the New Job Market, but it cannot, by itself, ensure that your record will match with any of the employment opportunities for which it is recruiting. To make as many of those connections as possible, you must use a resume that presents your qualifications in such a way that it is easy for the job bank's **computer** to recognize and understand them. Otherwise, you'll be plugged into the job bank's position vacancies, but not turned on to them.

Now, don't worry. You won't have to etch your occupational record onto a computer chip to produce an electronic resume. You also won't have to copy your credentials onto a computer disk, if you don't want to. In fact, you don't even have to know how to use a computer to be able to write an electronic resume.

COMPUTER FRIENDLY RESUMES

Your electronic resume is simply a modified version of your conventional paper resume. This new design, however, enables your resume to be stored and updated efficiently in a computer, read effectively by the computer's software and then extracted accurately from that computer, so that it can be forwarded to a prospective employer. In addition, as you will learn in just a moment, this new design also has important advantages with the human reviewers of resumes. It increases the impact of your resume by making your key qualifications easy to identify and understand by overworked recruiters. Hence, in many respects, an electronic resume is the supercharged, high technology version of your paper resume.

Although an electronic resume doesn't have blinking lights or whirring circuits, it is **very** different from a conventional paper resume, in both format and substance. These differences are driven by the fact that computers are very single-minded. Unlike humans, they cannot make judgments or extrapolate from the information you provide. You cannot count on them to read between the lines or to assume something on your behalf. For a computer, either what you want to say is there in a way the computer can recognize it or it's not. There are no "sort of's" or "maybe's."

The key to communicating with a computer, therefore, is to express your employment credentials (a) in clear, unadorned, straight forward language that conveys exactly what you mean and (b) in a format that highlights the key points so that even a computer can't miss them. An electronic resume integrates both of these components into an unique "computer friendly" design that can put the power of the job bank to work for you.

THE PERFECT RESUME

In effect, an electronic resume is similar to an old fashioned Position Wanted ad, only better. It puts your credentials into circulation continuously and confidentially, saving you both time and money. Even more important, an electronic resume has all of the information necessary to **match you with genuine employment opportunities** in the New Job Market. As a result, an electronic resume operates as a perpetual position finder.

It is the perfect job search tool for:

- **Job seekers**, those who are out of work and looking for a new job:
- **Job changers**, those who are currently employed, but seeking a different or better job; and
- **Job lookers**, those who are evaluating alternative career paths and employment opportunities generally.

Equally as important, an electronic resume is a job search tool that can help everyone, regardless of their occupational field. In the past, job banks worked best with positions in technical, scientific and other specialized fields because the qualifications for such fields were relatively detailed and specific and hence easy to store and identify in a computer. Today, however, as high definition jobs become the norm in virtually every field of work, an electronic resume is an effective way to connect with employment opportunities in every profession, craft and trade. At Job Bank USA, for example, we have used the electronic resumes of individuals in our data base to match them with open jobs in human resources management and training, sales and marketing, health care, customer service, general management, engineering, finance and accounting, management information systems, and equipment operation and maintenance.

Moreover, this unique design of electronic resumes also gives them an important versatility in the New Job Market. Indeed, electronic resumes have much broader applications than their use in job banks. For example, the advancing capability of technology and the decreased staffing available in the Human Resource Departments of many employers have stimulated a movement toward automation in recruiting. As a result, a number of employers, primarily large corporations, now use computer-based applicant tracking systems to manage the resumes they receive from individuals seeking employment. In essence, the computer has become the co-worker of the recruiter.

These systems have many of the characteristics of a job bank. In fact, their hardware and software operate in a fashion virtually identical to that of the larger commercial job banks. The occupational records of job applicants are scanned into a computerized data base maintained by the employer. When a position vacancy subsequently occurs in the employer's organization, the data base is searched by the computer to identify the records of those individuals who are qualified and eligible for further evaluation. Hence, an electronic resume can help you stand out and be noticed among the growing number of companies using computer-based applicant tracking systems, as well.

Even more broadly, the decreased staff resources available to employers, in general, and to their Human Resource Departments, in particular, has meant that resumes received from employment candidates get less and less time and attention. Increasingly, resumes are reviewed by a support staff person who must rapidly sort through a large pile of records to identify those individuals who are most likely to be qualified for a particular position vacancy and hence worthy of further consideration. As a result, some experts now estimate that a resume receives as little as 45 seconds attention when it reviewed! If it doesn't catch the attention of the staff person then, the window of opportunity is likely to slam shut for the candidate.

As you will shortly learn, an electronic resume provides an effective solution to this situation, as well. It gets the most important aspects of your credentials up front, where they are less likely to be overlooked. Unlike a conventional resume, it leads with your strengths rather than burying your credentials in the dense text of the body of your resume, so that even an overworked staff person can't miss them.

Hence, the substance and format of an electronic resume puts you in an advantageous position:

- In the job banks used by employers in the New Job Market,
- In the applicant tracking systems used inside employers' organizations, and
- With the recruiters and their support staff as they conduct their initial evaluation of employment candidates.

Whether it's single-minded computers or overworked staffers, an electronic resume has the right stuff, provided, of course, that it includes the right substance in the right format. The next two chapters will introduce these two important elements in detail.

7

ELECTRONIC RESUME FORMAT

*T*wo factors strongly influence the format of an electronic resume. One deals with what happens **before** a computer searches a data base to identify the resume of a prospective job candidate, while the other determines what happens **after** the computer does its work. Between those two points—when the computer is actually being used to evaluate the resumes of individuals who are qualified for a job—it is the substance of an electronic resume that is most important. (The next chapter addresses this subject in detail.) Nevertheless, your resume will never get you to that evaluation stage, unless you pay careful attention to what happens **before** and **after** it. The format of your resume is critically important at both of those two points.

THE IMPORTANCE OF "BEFORE"

Before a computer in an electronic job bank can read and evaluate your resume for position vacancies, the resume must be entered into a data base. As noted earlier, most electronic job banks and most employers with computerized applicant tracking systems use scanners and optical character recognition software to transfer resumes into their data base. Scanners, however, are very fickle machines. They can translate your resume into the language a computer will understand **only** if they can recognize and digest the words on your resume. The best way to ensure that a scanner will accept your resume is to lay it out in a format that is easy for the scanner to read. In other words, you want your electronic resume to be "computer friendly." Therefore, the first step in writing a good electronic resume is to incorporate the following guidelines into the format design of your resume.

LENGTH

An electronic resume should be limited to two pages in length. Some electronic job banks will accept more (e.g., Job Bank USA accepts two complete resumes from each candidate, but prefers that each resume be limited to two pages), but all job banks are trying to maximize the efficiency of their data bases. Long winded resumes tie up more than their fair share of the computer, so limit yours to two pages, if at all possible.

An electronic resume should not be printed front-to-back on a single piece of paper. Instead, print the pages of the resume on two separate sheets of paper. That way, the job bank can stack one page on top of the other and scan both pages of your resume into the computer at the same time. A resume that is printed on a single piece of paper, on the other hand, has to be scanned twice; once, for the front side, and a second time for the back side, and that duplication of effort slows the processing of your credentials.

To ensure that the two pages of your resume stay together during processing and in the computer, identify each as follows:

- Top or first page—Insert your name and contact information at the top of the page and centered, as shown below.

James Q. Seeker
1106 North Spring Field Drive
Allentown, Pennsylvania 66026
705-874-3302

- Bottom or second page—Insert your name and Page Two at the top of the page at the left hand margin, as shown below.

James Q. Seeker
Page Two

Use a paper clip to hold the two pages of your resume together. Do not use staples. Some scanners struggle with the holes and tears created when the staples are removed, as they must be for processing.

PAPER AND INK—I

Don't bother with expensive heavy weights or colors of paper. For an electronic resume, the best paper color is white; the best ink is black. They provide the greatest contrast which, in turn, helps the scanner to recognize the letters and words on your resume. Remember, a computer cannot make guesses about what it sees, so blurs and smudges look like indecipherable gobbledygook. For example, if you use blue or gray paper and black ink for your resume, it may look attractive to the human eye, but it presents an incredible challenge to the myopic computer. And when it translates the word "engineer" on your resume into "enjunioneer" in the data base, the computer won't understand. It thinks you are an "enjunioneer" and will certainly identify your resume for any job calling for **that** credential, but it will **not** identify you for a job as an engineer.

To appreciate just how much a scanner's inability to read your resume can hurt you, take a look at the resume that follows. The individual it describes might be a very accomplished person, but the computer will never recognize that fact. As a result, the computer will never identify him/her as qualified for a position and the value of an electronic job bank has been lost.

M@LVN e. OPR@
44 Hunt David Avenue
Raleigh, NC 55062
(313) 422-6646

OBJECTIVE: d and MBA education.
nameering backgroun
Obtain a position with a company that utilizes my e

QuALIEFICATIONS:
Two years expen'eiice as production eiigmeer *Ln a large petrochenu'ral plant
n @rorimental treatment systems design
Two years expenence as process engineer in e VI cess markets
Two years expen'ence as industn'al marketing manager m OEK distributor, and
cherru'ca pro
Excellent Interpersonal and conunuru'cations skills; reconunended for future
supervisory and leadership positions
N113A education with emphasis on production management and'mdustn'al
marketing

PROFESSIONAL F XPERI LENCE:
Marketing Manager; PA CLON GAS COMPANY; St. Louis, MO; 1992 Present
Participated on @gh performance, self directed work team that commercialized
new catal@c activated carbon
product line within eight months. Planned sales to exceed $10 MM in 1994.
Managed OEM, distn@butor, and chenu*cal process markets totaling $45 MM
in sales.
Developed marketing program targeted at hydrogen purification OEMs reswting
in $1 MM in sales to date.
Conducted ten new product feasibility studies; six studies were pursued for
further development.
Published two gas refinement tec@cal papers; presented both papers at national
trade shows.

Refinery Engineer; PA CLON GAS COMPANY; St. Loous, MO; 1990 1992
DesiVied, started up, and provided operator training for 20+ carbon adsorption
systems for van@ous air and
groundwater clean up applications.
Designed @and managed manufacture of 40+ mobile vapor phase adsorber U4
*ts, each val at $75,000.
.ru ued
Provided troubleshooting and recommendations for adsorber related customer
problems.
Conducted technical and safety training for intemal engineering and operations
personn I,.,.

Production Engineer; DUPONT CHEMICAL USA; Wilmington, DE; 1988
1990
Directed operations personnel, schedwed eqw'pment maintenance, and planned
shutdown pr *acts for 100 MM
Oi
gallon per year benzene production facility.
Engineered two process optii ru'zation pr @ects that resldted'm annual
sav@Lngs of $3.2 NM.
Oi
Implemented SPC prograi ns on four distillation towers; annual benzene
production grew by 2.1 MM gallons.
@aged detailed enginesting, construction, and start up of $3.1 @ waste
hydrocarbon coll@on system for
reduction of plant waste and coi npliajice with plant outfall pe@tting.

EDUCATION:
M.B.A., UNIVERSITY OF ST LOUIS; St. Louuis, MO; May 1994
Cw,nulative GPA . 3.2 4.0

B.S., OHI[O STATE UNI[VERSITY; State University, OH; 1987
Major . Cheii u*cal Eng'Lneeriiig
Cw nulative GPA: 3.6 4.0

COMPUTER:
Proficient use of mainframe and PC ba@ platfonns experienced va@th many
simldation optinu"zation, and statistical
software packages including Lotus 1 2 3, FORTRAN, @tab, ASPEN, and
various Windows based apptica@ons.

AFFILIATIONS:
Society of Soft Dn@nk Technolo 'sts; Gas Quality @ociation

CERTIEFICATIONS:
Eii 'neer In Training, 1990

PAPER AND INK-II

If possible, have your resume printed at a local copy shop. If that's not feasible, use a laser printer to print it out from your personal computer or word processor. The goal is to get good, clean black letters on the paper of your resume. The darker and more solid the letters, the better. Do not use a typewriter or a dot matrix printer, as the letters most such machines produce are not of adequate clarity or definition for scanners.

For the same reason, always send **an original copy** of your resume to a job bank. Do not submit your resume by facsimile machine. While that strategy will get it to the job bank or the employer more quickly than the mail, your resume is virtually impossible to scan once it arrives and most organizations simply can't afford the time to type it into the computer for you. So, what happens? Either it will be scanned as is, with the unfortunate results shown earlier, or it will be returned to you with the request that you re-type it. The end result is a delay in your electronic networking and potentially a degradation in your ability to connect to the employment opportunities available through the job bank.

The best paper weight for an electronic resume is copy grade paper (20 lb.) or something slightly heavier, such as off set printing grade paper (60 lb.). There are two reasons for this guideline. First, heavy paper may impress human recruiters, but they bother job banks. Some scanners will choke on heavier weights of paper, while others are forced to process it more slowly. Hence, the safest course is simply to avoid using it, altogether. Second, the resumes of qualified candidates are often copied for circulation within a prospective employer's organization. In effect, the money you spend on the higher grade paper is lost the minute you become a viable candidate. At best, that investment will influence only one person, and that's the original reviewer. Beyond that point, the weight and color of your resume's paper stock play virtually no role in the selection process. So, don't waste the money on fancy grades or colors of paper. Save it for your victory celebration after you've been offered the job!

Finally, most scanners can accept irregular sizes of paper, but some scanners cannot. Therefore, play it safe and use standard 8 1/2 x 11 inch paper for your electronic resume. When you send it off to the job bank, send it **unfolded and flat** in a large envelope. The creases created when you fold a resume to insert it into a smaller, business envelope can destroy the clarity of the lettering on even a high grade copy shop product.

TYPEFACE AND GRAPHICS

The best typefaces for an electronic resume are those in which the letters are clearly separated one from another. When letters run together, either because of the style of the typeface or its size, a scanner will have problems reading them. Therefore, use a typeface that gives you distinct and separate lettering, such as Helvetica or Times. The best font sizes are 12 to 14 points. They create letters that are large enough for most scanners to read and interpret, but not so large as to waste the limited space you have on your resume.

For the same reason, you should avoid most of the graphical techniques used in conventional resumes to catch the attention of human reviewers. The scanner works best with simplicity so avoid the use of:

Technique	Problem in Electronic Resumes
italics, underlining, fancy typefaces	Scanners need clear, distinct characters or they will see blots and blurs rather than letters.
columns or any other kind of landscaping	Scanners read from left to right, so columns look like different pages on the same page to a scanner; also diagrams and pictures can confuse scanners, because these devices are designed primarily to read text.
shading	Scanners need clear contrast between letters and background, so shading increases the likelihood of errors in reading by a scanner.
boxes	Scanners are confused by the vertical lines in boxes which they may read as the letter "l".

On the other hand, virtually all scanners can accept and understand bold lettering, so it is acceptable to use that one technique. As you will see below, however, I recommend that you confine your use of bold typeface to the titles of the major sections in your resume where it will enhance the appeal of your resume once it is assessed by the recruiters and hiring managers for a particular position vacancy. On the other hand, I don't think the use of bold typeface is helpful in the text of your resume. Its only role there would be to emphasize an aspect of your resume, and scanners and computers are immune to such techniques. Those single-minded devices read words, and whether they are bold or not will have absolutely no bearing on their recognition of the word or its importance.

So, let's summarize the guidelines for the format of your electronic resume, that are dictated by the computer-based processing it must survive to be effective:

- Two pages in length; each page on a separate sheet of paper identified with your name.

- 20-60 lb., 8½" x 11" white paper and black ink.

- Use original copies only, reproduced at a local copy shop or printed by laser printer.

- 12-14 point fonts in Helvetica or Times typeface.

- Careful use of bold lettering, but no italics, underlining, shading, boxes, columns or fancy graphics.

If you follow these guidelines, your electronic resume will have no problem being read and understood by the scanner used by an electronic job bank or by an employer with a computer-based applicant tracking system. Having taken these precautions, what does your resume look like once it has been satisfactorily digested by a computer?

THE IMPORTANCE OF "AFTER"

The amount of memory used by job banks to store electronic resumes on their computers is limited to one degree or another. Memory—or the available space in a data base—costs money. Consequently, most electronic job banks use their scanners and optical character software technology to process candidate resumes into the computer in the tightly compacted format shown on pages 49 and 50. This format takes up the minimum amount of memory possible in the computer and improves the efficiency with which the computer can search the

þ ®®BRIAN C. STONE 510 221 Apple Orchard Road Monterey, CA (520) 666 3321 ®®SUMMARY OF QUALIFICATIONS Fifteen years of successful sales and marketing management experience in health care, telecommunications and financial insurance industries Ability to quickly acquire thorough knowledge of products in virtually any industry Experienced in entrepreneurial enterprises Outstanding communication, organization and time management skills Strong interpersonal skills and ability to relate equally well to individuals at all levels of corporate structure ®®High levels of professionalism, integrity and dedication Strong work ethic initiative ®®EXPERIENCE Central Podiatry Center, Sacramento, CA. 5

91 Present Marketing Manager Establish and maintain physician accounts for podiatry centers Develop and execute market strategy for Sacramento and San Jose locations ®®Manage and maintain the operations Sacramento center ®®Increased Sacramento center's production by 25% within the first three months ®®Assisted in establishing new market center in Los Angeles location ®®MCI, San Diego, CA. 6 88 5 91 Sr. Account Executive, So. Calif. Branch ®®Recruited for position by Manager ®®Design and execute own market strategy ®®Rank in top 10% of sales among sixty colleagues in branch ®®Page 2 ®®Sell and maintain business accounts in several southern California counties, including Orange County and San Diego County ®®Spent initial month in intensive corporate training program and marketing program ®®Nationwide Insurance Company San Diego, CA. 6 85 6 88 Agent Registered Representative ®®Ranked in top 10% among 500 new agents nationwide and was invited to membership in "Scaling the Heights Nationwide Conference" ®®Attained Star Performers Level of 1986 production (top 10% of entire sales force) ®®Made California Educational Conference and Regional Sales Conference in 1987 ®®Marketed and sold life and disability insurance and equities to business and individual markets ®®Held 6, 63, 23 Security License ®®The Home Design Place, Costa, CA, 7 87 7 89 Partner General Manager ®®Established and operated profitable interior decorating business (installation and maintenance of customer service and sales centers for business establishments) ®®Major clients included AT&T, Hughes, Price Club, and Qwick Copy franchises as well as major hospitals, area restaurants, law and electronic firms ®®Developed and implemented market plan and strategy ®®Held total personnel administrative responsibilities for all employees ®®Sold business to partner after relocation to Sacramento area ®®Sunshine Products, Inc, Covina, Ca. 1982 1985 Distributor, Sacramento region ®®Owned and operated this successful distributorship of vitamins and healthcare products, sold exclusively to independent health food stores ®®Ranked first among twenty distributors nationwide ®®Prospected, sold and maintained client base of 200 stores, building excellent rapport and high volume sales ®®Page 3 ®®Capably executed purchasing, inventory, marketing, sales, recordkeeping, shipping and receiving functions; recognized as Entrepreneur of the Year by Independent Business Association ®®Distributorship dissolved when parent company changed exclusively to telemarketing sales ®®Other Experience ®®Calafrasis National Bank, Manager Assistant 1980 1982 ®®Dr. Jane Louiston, Office Manager 1979 1980 ®®EDUCATION ®®The California

State University, Fullerton, CA. Masters of Management Business Administration Emphasis June 1990 ®®The California State University, Fullerton, CA. Bachelor of Science May 1980 Graduated with distinction and complete requirements for majors in Business, Health Management and Biology Invited to membership in Epsilon Delta and Lakonians National Honor Societies ®þ

data base for prospective candidates. In other words, it has "less distance" to travel in order to read each of the resumes in the data base to identify those candidates who qualify for a particular position vacancy.

As you can see, all of the fancy spacing and lettering many people use on their resumes is eliminated by the process which electronic resumes must endure. So, does that mean that the visual appearance of an electronic resume is not important? Absolutely not! As noted at the outset of this chapter, the format of your resume plays a role **before** the computer reads it and evaluates it for a job search—during its scanning and processing into the job bank's data base—and **after** the computer has read and identified it for a position vacancy.

In other words, once the computer has been used to locate your resume (because it describes qualifications specified by an employer), the resume will be extracted from the data base and enter a conventional evaluation process. At that point, recruiters and hiring managers will conduct an assessment of what you can do and how well you can do it. To facilitate this review and show your credentials off to best advantage, your electronic resume must also be arranged to appeal to human eyes and tastes, as well as to the electronic gizmo's in the computer.

The format on the page 53 provides the best arrangement that satisfies both of these objectives. It uses the following techniques:

- Major section titles are set off in bold and all capital letters.

- Major subsections are set off in bold and initial capital letters (i.e., the first letter only in each word is capitalized).

- Accomplishments are set off and highlighted with bullets.

- A Key Word Preface begins your resume with a tight, complete summary of your occupational credentials.

- The Experience section, detailing your occupational background, immediately follows your Key Word Preface, unless you are a recent school/college graduate. The tasks you executed, the responsibilities you discharged and the achievements you accomplished in your work background are your most important qualifications for a new or better job.

- Sections describing your Education and Professional Affiliations & Awards follow the Experience section and conclude your resume.

- No space is wasted with personal data or with such obvious statements as "References furnished upon request." The personal data leaves you vulnerable to biases and prejudices which, although illegal, still exist. The references statement, on the other hand, uses space on your resume to say something that every recruiter already knows. It's very unlikely that you will be offered a job without references, so every qualified candidate, by definition, has them.

If you're a recent school/college graduate, however, and don't have such a track record, you should place your Education section in front of your Experience section, so as to highlight the **currency** of your occupational knowledge. **Your** most important qualification for that first job out of school is your exposure to and familiarity with the most up-to-date techniques, theory and principles in your field. Please note, however, that work experience, particularly in your field, is also **very** important for a recent school/college graduate. Indeed, a growing number of employers are hiring the recent graduates who interned with them during their education.

The following format is clean, clear and crisp. It lays out your credentials in a business-like arrangement that is easy on the eye, effective and efficient in its use of space. The next chapter will detail the substance of an electronic resume that will bring this format to life for both a single-minded computer and an overworked recruiter.

Your Name
Your Address
The Telephone Number at which you would like to be contacted

KEY WORD PREFACE:

This section of your resume contains the key words that a computer must see in your resume to consider you a qualified candidate for a specific position vacancy. A complete introduction to the Key Word Preface is provided in the next chapter.

EXPERIENCE:

Most Recent or Current Employer   Dates of Employment

Title of Your Most Recent Position   Dates in that position
Describe the knowledge, skills and abilities you currently use or demonstrated in this position, in a three to five sentence paragraph.

- List one-to-three accomplishments, setting each off separately with bullets. Bullets must be filled in and dark. Scanners will read hollow bullets as the letter "o."

**Title of Your Next Most Recent Position with
the Same Employer**   Dates in that position
Describe the knowledge, skills and abilities you demonstrated in this position, in a three to five sentence paragraph.

- List one-to-three accomplishments, setting each off separately with bullets. Bullets must be filled in and dark. Scanners will read hollow bullets as the letter "o."

NEXT MOST RECENT EMPLOYER   Dates of employment

Title of the Last Position You Held with That Employer   Dates in that position
Repeat the format above.

Title of the Next Most Recent Position with That Employer   Dates in that position
Repeat the format above.

EDUCATION:

List your degrees, certificates, most important occupational training and licenses in this section.

PROFESSIONAL AFFILIATIONS & AWARDS:

List all of your professional activities, to include the professional and trade organizations to which you belong and any awards or recognition you have received from these groups.

8

ELECTRONIC RESUME SUBSTANCE

*T*he unique computer-based processing and handling techniques of a job bank dictate a special design for the format of an electronic resume. Without that format, the document cannot be efficiently or accurately entered into the computer and hence may lose the special advantages of electronic networking.

The substance of your electronic resume is every bit as critical to its success in the employment hyperspace of the New Job Market. Indeed, it is the substance of your resume that determines its ability to identify and highlight your credentials in the computerized data base of a job bank. Without the right substance, the connections are broken between the employment opportunities of the job bank and your qualifications for those positions. As a result, your resume gathers electronic dust in the computer, and you lose the value and benefit of a job bank.

THE IMPORTANCE OF KEY WORDS

The substance of your electronic resume is shaped by the way computers read text, in general, and resumes, in particular. Computers read resumes by looking for key words. These key words are normally nouns or short phrases. They describe the knowledge, skills, abilities and experience that the employer must see in a person's resume to consider him or her a qualified candidate for an open position. When an employer asks a job bank to search its data base for employment candidates, the key words are obtained either from a position description or from an interview with the recruiter or hiring manager. Some of the key words will be designated as requirements, without which a person cannot be a qualified candidate, while others may be considered capabilities that the employer would like to see in a candidate, but are not a precondition to hiring.

An electronic resume, therefore, is designed to present your occupational credentials using as many key words as possible. To get a feel for the key words that an employer might want to see in your resume, check the recruitment ads for your field of work in your local newspaper. Look at the specific terms that employers have used to describe the knowledge, skills, abilities, competencies, capabilities, experience and background required for employment candidates in your field. Alternatively, you can review the position descriptions that most employers maintain for the jobs in their organization. These documents are usually filed in the Human Resource Department and may even be posted for position vacancies.

In addition, you can check with an executive recruiter or "head hunter" who specializes in your field. If he/she has conducted one or more searches recently for a position or positions similar to yours, the criteria for those searches will give you a detailed vocabulary of the most current key words in your field. Finally, you should check with your professional or technical association. If there is a certification or professional education and advancement program in that organization, it is likely to have instructional or testing objectives which will also give you an insight into the key words of importance in your field.

Of course, your resume should include only those key words that describe qualifications that you actually have. In fact, think of key words as terms which describe your **ASSETS**. They are nouns or short phrases used to present the **value** you offer to an employer. They include:

ABILITIES—Any learned or acquired capability, expertise, knowledge, skill or competency that will enable you to perform your job at an exceptional level. Key words for Abilities might include Budget Management, Operations Research/Systems Analysis, AS 4000 Programming, Oral & Written Communications Skills, Team Building, Sales Prospecting and IBM Word Processing.

SPECIAL AWARDS AND RECOGNITION—Any recognition which you've received on the job or from your professional association that would indicate a special level of expertise, experience or commitment. Key words for Awards might include Sales Leader Award, Quality Control Supervisors Award, MIS Department Outstanding Performance Certificate, and National Management Association/Distinguished Service Award.

SPECIAL LICENSES AND CERTIFICATIONS—Any formal designation or title which you have earned via study, test, evaluation or other review process conducted by your college or university, professional association, state or federal government or other recognized institution. Key words for special licenses & certifications might include SPHR (Senior Professional in Human Resources), CFP (Certified Financial Planner), Cum Laude Graduate, and Professional Engineer License Number 123445.

EXPERIENCE—Your years of experience in your occupational field or industry, or your management/ skill level as well as any unique background with special projects, responsibilities, and activities. Key words for Experience might include 14 Years in Plastic Industry, All Functions in Corporate Finance, Chairman for Special Environmental Compliance Project, 5 Years in Computer Sales and Administrative Assistant to Corporate Executives.

TRAINING—Any program of learning relevant to your performance in your field, to include high school, vocational school, college, in-house training and special educational programs. Key words for Training might include Master of Science in Structural Engineering, Motorola Total Quality Management Training, Associate of Arts in Administrative Science, Continuing Education in Spanish, Formal Training in Statistical Process Control, and Stanford Executive Development Course.

SYNONYMS—different people and organizations use different words to say the same thing. To account for this variability in human expression, your key words should include any alternative words, phrases or acronyms used to describe any of the key words in your resume. Illustrative key word synonyms are Personnel Administration for Human Resource Management, MA for Masters of Arts, Association or Society for Not-For-Profit, Attorney for Lawyer, and Director or Supervisor for Manager.

Key words present your assets in terms used by employers. Why? Because those are the words and phrases employers provide to job banks for their data base searches. If you have the right skill, but describe it with the wrong word, you'll be overlooked by the computer. It's as simple as that. So, there are only two criteria for selecting which key words to include in your resume:

1. They must be an accurate, honest expression of your qualifications and

2. They must be the words and phrases **used by employers** to describe your qualifications.

Given these two criteria, several additional guidelines for developing the key words for your electronic resume follow:

- It's perfectly all right to use acronyms in an electronic resume. If employers use the acronym to describe a required qualification, then it should appear in the resume. A word of caution is in order, however. If the acronym and its complete term are used interchangeably by employers, then **both** should appear in the resume.

- It's okay to use jargon and detailed technical terms in an electronic resume, if employers use such words to describe required qualifications in your field.

- You should avoid the use of soft, inexact or flowery language in an electronic resume. Employers do not use such terms as "empowerment," "streamlined," and "shirt sleeves manager" as key words when identifying the required qualifications for a position vacancy. These terms may make for pleasant reading, but they do not add important information to the resume and hence do not contribute to your evaluation by a computer.

THE KEY WORD PREFACE

As we discussed in the previous chapter, an electronic resume begins with a Key Word Preface. The Key Word Preface is a new technique specifically designed for an electronic resume. It operates as your own personalized "electronic business card" for electronic networking. In other words, it is the way you introduce yourself to many of the employers in the New Job Market, whom you don't know, but whom you want to know **you**.

The Key Word Preface is a critical component of your resume for two very important reasons:

1. A growing number of resumes are being entered into computers by optical character recognition technology and

2. Resumes are increasingly read by single-minded computers and overworked staff persons.

Even a resume with very strong content, one which includes all of the key words that describe your occupational credentials, can be overlooked, if the format of the document doesn't address the impact of these two factors. Consequently, the key words in an electronic resume should be organized into two sections. The first is a Key Word Preface; the second is the main body of your resume.

The Key Word Preface appears directly beneath your name and contact information at the top of the first page of your resume. It is an inventory of your most important assets, as described by the key words you expect employers to use to describe your qualifications. The Key Word Preface is a list that runs twenty to thirty principal items in length, not including articles and conjunctions such as "the," "and," "&," or "of." A principal item is the key word or phrase that describes a single qualification. The first letter of each word in the item is capitalized and the entire item is followed by a period. For example:

KEY WORD PREFACE: Human Resource Management and Development. Ten Years Experience in Health Care Industry. Compensation & Benefits. Employee Relations. Staffing. Union Relations. EEO/AA. Succession Planning. Vice President of Human Resources for 1,000 Employee Company. SPHR.

The Key Word Preface acts as an inventory of the assets you can bring to an employer and as an advertisement about the quality of those assets. As an inventory, it includes the words that a computer or a recruiter must see to consider you a qualified candidate for a position vacancy. Basically, these words and phrases detail three aspects of your background:

- Your skills, abilities and competencies

- Your experience using those skills, abilities and competencies, and

- Your accomplishments in using those skills, abilities and competencies on-the-job.

As an advertisement, the Key Word Preface is right up front where it can't be ignored or overlooked. It has the right words for a single-minded computer and the right location for an overworked recruiter. Hence, the Key Word Preface effectively and efficiently tells an employer **what you can do** and **how well you can do it**.

Following the Key Word Preface, the body of an electronic resume should be organized into three sections: Experience, Education, and Professional Affiliations and Awards. Each of these sections is described in detail below.

EXPERIENCE

As with the Key Word Preface, the Experience section is an opportunity for you to document your on-the-job performance. Hence, I believe that the best format for this section is a hybrid of the chronological and functional formats used in conventional resumes. The chronological format arranges your credentials according to your work history and presents them in chronological order, usually beginning with the most recent and working backwards to the most distant. A functional format, on the other hand, presents the occupational qualifications you possess and the experience you have had in building and using those capabilities.

Both of these formats have certain strengths and weaknesses. A chronological resume does a good job of detailing your work experience, but may not provide adequate visibility to the knowledge, skills and abilities you demonstrated in each position. The functional resume clearly overcomes that problem, but also makes it very difficult to determine what positions you have held, in what order and during which periods of time.

The hybrid format is widely used in conventional resumes because it eliminates many of these shortcomings, while capturing the best features of the other two formats. A hybrid format clearly presents your work history in chronological order and the knowledge skills, and abilities that you demonstrated in each position. Hence, its only drawback is that you may not have the space, given the length constraints of resumes, to cover every one of your prior work positions in detail. Nevertheless, I strongly recommend that you use the hybrid format because it best enables you to highlight your capabilities and experience in the key words that a single-minded computer and an overworked recruiter will recognize and understand.

Indeed, showcasing your capabilities is the single most important purpose of the Experience section. Remember, organizations, today, are challenged by unprecedented competition in domestic and international markets and by escalating demands for improved productivity, quality assurance and customer satisfaction. To meet these challenges, employers seek workers who can demonstrate that they have both the background and the motivation to excel. Organizations, today, want to hire winners, because they know that their survival rides on the quality and commitment of their workers. The Experience section is the place in your resume where you can prove that you have this kind of background, that you have the right stuff.

The hybrid format organizes your experience around the progression of your employment positions, in reverse chronological order. In other words, the section describes each of the jobs you've held during your career, beginning with the most recent first. Jobs are arranged by employer, so the name of each of your employers and the dates you worked there are listed first. Then, the title of each of the positions that you held with that employer and the dates you held them are presented. As shown below, names and titles are entered from the left hand margin, while dates are entered from the right. The names of your various employers serve as major section headings, so they should appear in all capital letters and bold type face. Position titles will then appear beneath the corresponding employer's name, in initial capital letters (i.e., the first letter of each word is capitalized) and bold type face.

RESEARCH DYNAMICS CORPORATION	01/90-03/94
Department Manager	06/92-03/94
Regional Sales Manager	01/90-06/92

This format enables you to provide additional information about **what you can do** and **how well you can do it,** that you summarized in the Key Word Preface.

What You Can Do

Beneath each position title, present a mini-work history that showcases the capabilities you demonstrated in this job, using the key words that single-minded computers and overworked recruiters will recognize and understand.

Limit yourself to a paragraph of three-to-five clear, hard-hitting statements. Don't talk about responsibilities—talk about capabilities. Hence, each sentence will identify either the major tasks you performed on-the-job or the skills and abilities you used to accomplish those tasks. And, remember, the vocabulary you use in these statements must be the key words or their synonyms that you developed for your Key Word Preface. In effect, the Experience section is the place where you present the proof. It's your opportunity to describe and amplify the details of the knowledge, skills and abilities which you highlighted in the Preface.

That proof is critically important. Employers want to know what you **can do** for them. They hear a lot of claims and promises from job candidates, but not much of it gets taken very seriously. Instead, most organizations look for proof. They rely upon a very simple premise: if you've done something successfully in the past, you can probably do it again, maybe even better, in the future. Therefore, your "track record" of experience in the past is the single best way for you to impress an employer. Each and every statement in your resume is an advertisement about you. To be effective, that ad should adhere to several principles:

1. **It must be accurate and honest.** No exaggerations, no misleading suggestions and certainly no misstatements of fact.

2. **It should leave nothing to the imagination.** As far as the employer is concerned, you didn't do it, if you don't say so. That's particularly true of electronic resumes. Remember, they'll be read by a single-minded computer that can't read between the lines and can't make a guess on your behalf.

3. **Your ad should be written for your audience.** You want to be sure that the audience recognizes and understands what you're saying. For electronic resumes, that audience is a single-minded computer, and for all resumes, it is an overworked recruiter. Hence, your experience must be described using the key words and their synonyms for which computers and recruiters are looking.

By adhering to these principles, a good skills paragraph might look something like this:

Recruited, trained and directed six person sales team for leading plastics manufacturer. Conducted comprehensive market analysis to identify key customer opportunities in the region. Reorganized sales territories to eliminate overlaps and focus on key new clients. Devised innovative sales call and call back strategy to ensure agents developed effective customer relationships. Developed and personally implemented special handling procedures for all accounts in excess of $1 million.

Remember, the goal here is to describe your capabilities in short, hard hitting sentences that use the key words you think an employer will expect to see in the resume of any qualified candidate. However, as the paragraph above illustrates, the key words are neither presented in a laundry list nor enclosed in simple sentences that say nothing more than the fact you have such skills. In effect, your key word statements must also say something about what you **can do** with the capabilities and background those key words describe. For example, don't declare "I was responsible for the development of sales strategy." Instead say, "Devised innovative sales and call back strategy to ensure agents developed effective customer relations." Consequently, in the illustrative paragraph above, each sentence has two parts:

1. The key words themselves and

2. The experience you had with the capability they describe.

In addition, to be most effective, each key word statement should describe some improvement or contribution that was produced by your capabilities and actions. Remember, a prospective employer is looking for someone who can achieve beneficial results on-the-job. If you've been able to do that for one employer, there's a good chance you'll be able to do it for a new employer, as well. Each key word statement, then, should contain three elements:

1. A Key Word or Words

                        +

2. A statement of what you can do with them

                        +

3. Some benefit or improvement achieved by those actions.

The chart below identifies these three components in each key word statement in the illustrative paragraph presented earlier.

Key Words	**What You *Can Do* for Employers**
team, plastics (industry)	recruited, trained and directed **new sales team** in plastics industry
market analysis	conducted analysis and implemented results to identify opportunities for **greater sales**
new client (development)	**improved organization's ability** to focus on sales among new clients
strategy	developed and implemented innovative strategy to produce **better performance** among sales people

$1 million accounts	developed and personally implemented **improved procedures** for managing major accounts

In summary, each paragraph in your electronic resume that describes your experience in a particular job should highlight the key words that identify the knowledge, skills and abilities you demonstrated in that position, the tasks or activities you **can do** with those capabilities, and the benefit or improvement those actions produce. Such a paragraph will provide you with two important advantages:

1. It can be understood by single-minded computers and overworked recruiters and

2. It provides a meaningful description of your capabilities and their application on-the-job.

Those two benefits will help determine whether or not you are a qualified candidate for a particular position. They will not, however, differentiate you from the competition. They will not set you apart from all other qualified candidates who are also competing for an employer's open position. To do that, you have to describe your accomplishments at work. In other words, each key word paragraph in your resume—if it's written well—will tell the computer or recruiter what you **can do**; to that, you must add some evidence of **how well can you do it**.

How Well Can You Do It

Perhaps the best proof you can offer regarding your knowledge, skills and abilities is the record of accomplishments you have achieved in using those capabilities on-the-job. Accomplishments describe the successful application of your competencies in real world, work situations. They provide some insight about your motivation, commitment and degree of expertise. Most importantly, they indicate a level of performance that you have already achieved and hence should be able to repeat and build on for a new employer.

Accomplishments are so important that they should be set off from the text of your resume and highlighted for that single-minded computer and overworked recruiter. There are two steps you can take to do that. First, limit the number of accomplishments you present to no more than three per job you have held. A long laundry list of accomplishments diminishes the impact of any single one, so be selective. Pick the one, two, or three achievements that you feel best exemplify your unique capabilities and present those. Second, limit the description of each accomplishment to a single fact-filled statement. Wherever possible, include quantitative measures of your success in your statements. Such empirical "evidence" provides more credibility and impact for your accomplishment.

Insert each statement describing an accomplishment beneath the paragraph corresponding to the position in which it occurred and set it off by bullets. Therefore, an effective statement might look like this:

- Increased sales by 20% per year over the past two years.

  or

- Lowered turnover rate among sales agents by 46%.

  or

- Improved key account renewal rate by 15%.

All of these statements demonstrate a capability, a task or action you **can do** on-the-job *and* **how well you can do it**. As shown below, when these statements of accomplishment are amended to their corresponding key word paragraph, they produce a complete picture of your experience in a particular position that has genuine power and impact. It's a portrait of you and your capabilities that will be understood and appreciated by either a computer or a human recruiter.

RESEARCH DYNAMICS CORPORATION	01/90-03/94
Department Manager	06/92-03/94
Regional Sales Manager	01/90-06/92

Recruited, trained and directed six person sales team for leading plastics manufacturer. Conducted comprehensive market analysis to identify key customer opportunities in the region. Reorganized sales territories to eliminate overlaps and focus on key new clients. Devised innovative sales call and call back strategy to ensure agents developed effective customer relationships. Developed and personally implemented special handling procedures for all accounts in excess of $1 million.

- Increased sales by 20% per year for the past two years.

- Lowered turnover rate among sales agents by 46%.

- Improved key account renewal rate by 15%.

Each description of each job you have held should be described this way in the Experience section of your resume. This technique provides enough substance to attract the interest of a recruiter, in the key words that will be recognized by a computer. It allows you:

1. To qualify yourself as a candidate for a specific job opening by pointing out the principal knowledge, skills, and abilities you've used in your various jobs and by demonstrating your application of those capabilities in the tasks and activities of your work, and

2. To differentiate yourself from the competition by highlighting your accomplishments in performing those tasks and activities on-the-job.

As further evidence of your capabilities, the next section of your resume should detail your educational credentials.

EDUCATION

The Education section in an electronic resume must be more complete and detailed than the same section in a conventional resume. That's because recruiters typically cite more than formal degrees and certificates as key words for selecting qualified candidates. These additional key words cover a range of subjects, including (a) special training programs in such subjects as Total Quality Management and Statistical Process Control, Preventing Sexual Harassment, Working in Diverse Work Groups; (b) continuing educational experiences to acquire value-added skills in English oral and written communications, foreign language competency, and computer literacy; and (c) formal licenses and certifications.

All of these educational qualifications should be organized into an Education section with three integrated subsections:

- **First subsection**—the degrees and certificates you have earned from formal educational programs,

- **Second subsection**—the most significant training and continuing education experiences you have had during your career, and

- **Third subsection**—your formal credentials, licenses and certifications.

Recognizing that there is limited room for such information on your resume, I suggest that you keep a separate running record of **all** of it (so that you'll have it handy for your interviews) and select one-to-three items from each area for actual inclusion in your resume. To select these items, use the following criteria:

1. The more recent (the degree, training, or license), the better and

2. The higher (the degree, training or license), the better.

The first subsection lists all of the formal education degrees or certificates you have received, beginning with the most recent first. These credentials signify your successful completion of a specific educational experience which will, in turn, provide further confirmation to a recruiter or computer that you possess the specific knowledge, skills and abilities required for a vacancy. They also underscore your capacity to stay with an activity and to see it through to successful completion. In other words, those degrees and certificates also say something about your determination, your strength of character and your ability to get things done, all of which are important qualifications in today's demanding workplace.

List your degrees and certificates, beginning at the left hand margin. Then, identify the corresponding educational institution, spacing its name roughly in the center of the page. This arrangement (i.e., degree first, then school) is reversed from that usually suggested for conventional resumes for a very specific reason. The degree or certificate is the most common key word used to identify required educational experience for a position vacancy. As both humans and computers read from left to right, this arrangement puts the key words out, where they are most likely to be seen.

Identify your degree or certificate, using the most common key words for the degree (e.g., Masters in Public Administration, MPA, Masters in Business Administration, MBA, Doctor of Philosophy in Literature, Ph.D. in Literature, Associate of Arts, AA, Certificate in Paralegal Studies, High School Diploma, General Education Degree, GED). If you used the abbreviation in your Key Word Preface, then state the entire name for the degree in the Education section or vice versa. In addition, if you received the degree with honors (e.g., Cum Laude, Summa Cum Laude), this distinction should be included, as well.

Finally, indicate the date you received the degree, at the right hand margin. Some resume books will tell you to indicate the beginning date as well as the completion date of your degrees and certificates. While that information is nice to have, it takes up room on your resume and adds nothing of real importance to the credibility or strength of your credentials. In other words, the length of time you spent getting the degree is not nearly as important as how recent that degree is. The more recent the degree, the more up-to-date your skills, and that's precisely what the completion date will tell a recruiter or computer.

The first subsection should appear as follows:

EDUCATION:		
Masters in Public Administration	Harvard University	1979
Masters in Literature	Middlebury College	1978
Bachelors of Science	United States Military Academy	1971

The second subsection covers your most significant training and continuing education experiences. Your resume has greater strength if you indicate an on-going commitment to staying current in your primary occupational field and to gaining new skills that can expand your contribution and impact on-the-job. Indeed, today, employers are most impressed with people who look more like "works in progress" than "finished products," because they know that technology and strategies are evolving so rapidly that a person can only stay up-to-date if he/she is in school virtually all of the time.

This subsection in an electronic resume is your chance to show that you accept the responsibility for and are committed to life-long learning. If possible, it should list training programs you have completed and those in which you are still engaged. However, limit your list to those training programs and educational experiences that are relevant to your work on-the-job. This subsection is not the place to include that course in barn painting you took at the local community center, unless barn painting is important to your qualifications in your field of work. The best rule of thumb is to include an education experience **if** an employer is likely to identify the skill you acquire from that experience as a key word. How do you know? Check the newspaper recruitment ads and talk to headhunters in your field.

Once you've selected the programs to include in this section, list the subject or title of the course, beginning at the left hand margin. As with your formal degrees and certificates, the subject of your training is far more important to a prospective employer than where you took the course, so it is identified first. Then, state where the course was taken, spaced roughly in the center of the page, and the date it was completed, at the right hand margin. If you're still completing the course, state "On-going" where the date of completion would have been entered. For example,

---

EDUCATION:

Masters in Public Administration	Harvard University	1979
Masters in Literature	Middlebury College	1978
Bachelors of Science	United States Military Academy	1971
Spanish	Northern Virginia Community College	On-going
Total Quality Management	Motorola Quality Institute	1989

The final subsection of your Education identifies your formal licenses, certifications and other credentials that convey a specific level of expertise recognized and valued by your industry or profession. Normally, such credentials require the successful completion of a specified course of instruction and a certifying exam, conducted either by the profession's designated association, society or institute or by the state or federal government.

List your licenses or certifications at the left hand margin. Remember to use the key words you think an employer would use to identify these qualifications for a position vacancy. Then, roughly in the center of the page, identify

1. The state, institution or organization that awarded the license to you;

2. The number of your license, so that it can be confirmed by the employer; and

3. At the right hand margin, the date you received the license or the date it was most recently renewed. For example,

---

EDUCATION:

Masters in Public Administration	Harvard University	1979
Masters in Literature	Middlebury College	1978
Bachelors of Science	United States Military Academy	1971
Spanish	Northern Virginia Community College	On-going
Total Quality Management	Motorola Quality Institute	1989
Professional Engineers License	Virginia #123456	1980
Senior Human Resource Professional	SHRM #109876	1986

The Education section in an electronic resume has to do more "heavy lifting" than a corresponding section in a conventional resume. The use of key words to search for and identify qualified candidates requires that the section expand to include any other special knowledge, training, licenses and certifications you may have. In addition, such an approach to detailing your educational experience will make an important statement about your commitment to continuous personal development, which can, in and of itself, help to differentiate you from the competition.

PROFESSIONAL AFFILIATIONS AND AWARDS

This section is the last in your electronic resume. It details your level of involvement, your stature and your standing in your profession, craft or trade. These credentials are important because they provide further evidence of your competency and your commitment to excellence in what you do. Hence, this section should detail your activities involving your professional or trade association, but not your homeowner's association, unless the latter has something to do with your field of work.

In addition, this subsection should include your participation in more general organizations related broadly to your work (the Chamber of Commerce, Young President's Organization, American Management Association), but not your alumni association, your Bird Watcher's Club or the Parent-Teachers

Association. It may also include activities, events and accomplishments that are not related to a specific organization but which describe your on-going occupational development (professional papers and articles which you have published, speeches and workshops you have presented, independent projects you have completed).

In other words, limit entries in this section to those which are likely to

1. Be identified as a key word or

2. Provide additional evidence that will help to differentiate other key words in your resume.

Unlike the entries in the Education section, the names of the key professional or trade associations to which you belong should appear first in this section, beginning at the left hand margin. Given the wide range of possible levels of participation and recognition among these organizations, it is far more likely that the affiliation itself (i.e., the name of the organization) will be the key word used by either that single-minded computer or the overworked recruiter.

For each organization you list, identify any positions you've held (Chairman of the Education Committee, Member of the Board of Directors, Chapter Chairman) or special activities you undertook on its behalf (Chairman of the Annual Conference, Member of Ad Hoc Committee on Dues) and the dates you did so. Also identify any special awards or citations you've been given that would provide further evidence of your level of participation and recognition (Special Citation for Continuous Service) and their dates, as well. In the case of papers you've published or programs you've presented, cite the name of the publication or organization, the name of your paper or presentation in quotation marks and the appropriate dates. For example,

---

PROFESSIONAL AFFILIATIONS & AWARDS:

Society for Human Resource Management	Excellence in Education Award	1989
National Society for Performance & Instruction	"Training Generation X" workshop	1991
Authors Guild	Admitted as Member	1991
Training Magazine	"How to Make Training Pay"	1992

Membership in and awards from professional and technical organizations in your field and participation in other developmental organizations and experiences related to your work are important indications of your commitment to high caliber performance and excellence in your occupation. They convey qualities of character—a sense of purpose and a dedication to personal accomplishment—that are highly regarded by employers everywhere. Hence, they are fitting statements with which to close your resume.

Do not end your resume with the following types of statements often included on conventional resumes:

Personal References Available Upon Request

Why? The recruiter already knows that. In most cases, you won't be hired without them.

Married. Two Children. Member of Beth Shalom Temple. Episcopalian. Excellent Health, 52 years old. African American. Asian American. Caucasian Male. Female. Handicapped.

Why? These statements will almost never be key words for a position vacancy. They aren't relevant to your work, except in rare circumstances. Besides, they can inadvertently expose you to illegal prejudice or bias in your job search. It's not supposed to occur, but why take a chance?

Enjoy sailboating, swimming, horseback and riding, hunting, fishing, and so on. Active Republican/Democratic Party.

Why? Because they are hobbies non-occupational interests and therefore not relevant to your work. These interests may help you to build rapport with a recruiter, but the time and place for that is in an interview. When you're trying to get noticed by a single-minded computer, these statements aren't helpful because they will never be used as key words for a position vacancy and they take up scarce space on your resume.

The trick to writing a good electronic resume is to discipline yourself to include only those aspects of your qualifications that

1. Can be described in key words the computer will recognize or

2. Provide additional detail that will differentiate you from the competition for a position vacancy.

If you can do that, you'll have a resume with genuine power and impact, even in today's overcrowded and overheated job market.

Section IV

WRITE YOUR ELECTRONIC RESUME RIGHT

9

SAMPLE ELECTRONIC RESUMES— The Good, the Bad & the Ugly

*T*he following resumes illustrate some of the most important principles involved in writing an effective electronic resume. The Comments box at the end of each resume critiques the resume and points out its key strengths and weaknesses. None of these resumes are completely good or bad (or completely ugly). As with most resumes, each has its good points and bad points. They are presented solely to demonstrate the critical aspects of substance and format in an electronic resume.

Jane Alexander
52 Wakefield Street
Reston, Virginia 06735

(703) 771-5342 (Res)   (703) 776-3345 (Bus)

Objective

Position in Life Care / Nursing Facility Management where educational background,
practical experience and a commitment to provide dignity and high quality service to
residents will be utilized.

Education

UNIVERSITY OF CONNECTICUT, Bridgeport, CT
Master's Degree - Health Management (6/93)

PENNSYLVANIA STATE UNIVERSITY, University Park, PA
Bachelor of Science Degree - Business Administration (6/87)

NORTHERN VIRGINIA COMMUNITY COLLEGE, Sterling, VA
A.A.S. - Hotel Administration (6/77)

Experience

SUNRISE HOUSE, Reston, VA   6/87 - Present

Financial Services Administrator   5/91 - Present
*   Manage financial services and accounting practices for 200-bed skilled nursing facility.
*   Directly responsible for collections; successful in bringing collections debt down
    $100,000.
*   Conduct mid-month collection analysis.
*   Maintain accurate records of current financial status.
*   Prepare individualized monthly billing, electronic billing to State of Virginia, daily and
    monthly census, and cash deposits.
*   Prepare status reports on expired/discharged clients.
*   Directly accountable for accounts receivable and Medicaid billing.
*   Responsible for maintaining Medicare accounts (Parts A & B) as well as maintenance
    and collection of aged reports.
*   Process co-insurance cases.
Operations Supervisor   6/87 - 5/91
*   Managed and directed daily operations for facility serving 175-200 persons daily.
*   Supervised, scheduled and evaluated staff of 30+.
*   Responsibilities included purchasing, cost control, event planning, meal preparation,
    inventory control and quality assurance.
*   Ensured State health and sanitation regulations were strictly adhered to.
*   Coordinated policies and programs covering employee services and training.

FAIRFAX COMMUNITY COLLEGE, Arlington, VA   1/91 - Present

Associate Professor
Teach course work which includes: Introduction to Hospice Industry, Front Office
Operations (Personnel, Employee Relations, Accounting, Financial Reporting, Guest
Relations, Security Management, Computer Analysis, and Management Philosophy).

Licensure

Licensed Nursing Home Administrator - VA #007731

ANALYSIS:

Strengths

- The detailed list of activities under each position includes many key words.

- The inclusion of the person's license and its number are very important key words. However, the date of the license should be noted.

Weaknesses

- The use of an Objective rather than a Key Word Preface forces the reviewer to search for the person's qualifications in the body of the resume.

- The Education section should not appear in front of the Experience section, unless the person is a recent school/college graduate. The most important qualification for a mid career professional is her experience, so that section should appear first. The most important qualification for a recent school/college graduate is his/her up-to-date knowledge, so the Education section should appear first.

- The person's accomplishments (e.g., "bringing collections debt down $100,000") are buried in the text and hence difficult to find or notice. That, in turn, undermines their potential impact with reviewers.

- The use of italics will confuse the scanner at a job bank and degrade the processing of the resume.

- Misspelled words hurt the professional image of the individual and degrade the ability of the computer to identify her based on correctly spelled key words used by the employer.

James R. Johnston

Home: 412 331 8865   1707 Apple Avenue
Work: 412 772 4453   Philadelphia, Pennsylvania 15213

POSITION OBJECTIVE

Challenging Executive Management position in a progressive health care organization which seeks an individual with a diverse management background.

CAREER HISTORY

ST. LUKE'S HOSPITAL, VALLEY FORGE, PA   1990-Present

LOGISTIC DIRECTOR   Jan, 1990-Present

Responsible for the management of Purchasing, Storeroom, Shipping, Receiving and Supply Distribution for 300 bed primary care facility.

PITTSBURGH GENERAL HOSPITAL,
  PITTSBURGH, PA   1986-1990

MANAGER OF PROCUREMENT   July, 1989-Jan, 1990
MANAGER OF LOGISTICS SERVICES   Feb, 1986-July, 1989

Responsible for the management of Purchasing, Inventory Control, Receiving and Distribution, Linen Contract and Transport Escort Service for 250 bed primary care facility.

THE HOSPITAL OF ST. JUDE, PITTSBURGH, PA   1981-1986

DIRECTOR OF TRANSPORTATION AND SUPPLIES Aug, 1984-Feb, 1986
MANAGER OF ADMINISTRATIVE SERVICES   May, 1981-Aug, 1984

Responsible for the management of Supply Distribution, Mail Room, Linen Service, Transportation and Delivery Service and Housekeeping activity in the ancillary and clinic areas.

EDUCATION

THE INDIANA UNIVERSITY OF PENNSYLVANIA,
  LAUREL HILLS, PA   MAY, 1981

Bachelor of Science Degree in Health Planning and Administration.

Resume of James R. Johnston
Page 2

ACCOMPLISHMENTS

* Implemented new prime vendor contracts, resulting in cost savings of
  $545,000 over three years.

* Reduced Purchasing staff by 10%, decreased the volume of purchase orders
  by 30%, while improving service delivery levels.

* Negotiated and implemented a modular office systems contract, resulting in
  cost savings of $123,000 in the first year.

* Oversaw implementation of Total Quality Management process in the
  Purchasing Department, improving productivity and raising performance
  standards for the staff.

AFFILIATIONS

* Member, Hospital Purchasing and Materials Management Association

ANALYSIS:

Strengths

- The individual's accomplishments are clearly set apart and can be easily identified.

- A relatively wide array of key words, particularly industry, quantitative and functional terms, appear in his list of accomplishments.

- His name has been included on the second page of his resume so it can be identified if the second page gets separated during scanning and processing.

Weaknesses

- The use of an Objective rather than a Key Word Preface forces the reviewer to search for the person's qualifications in the body of the resume.

- The chronological format of the resume provides very little information about and few key words for the skills and abilities exercised by the individual in each of his positions.

- The separation of Accomplishments from positions in the Experience section makes it impossible to determine where these achievements occurred and when, undermining their impact on the reviewer.

- The lack of any additional education or training since 1981 hurts the individual's credibility as an up-to-date professional with an expanding set of skills and knowledge.

- The use of responsibility statements rather than descriptions of what the individual did and how well he did it in each position misses many of the key words necessary to match this person with a position vacancy.

JULIE M. BARTOW

7705 Georges Hall, P.O. Box 55   (903) 522 1963 (home)
Columbia, SC 27695-7487   (903) 753 8900 (office)

SUMMARY OF QUALIFICATIONS

Possess excellent supervisory skills; able to effectively lead, motivate, and inspire. Highly organized and energetic worker, able to manage many complex projects simultaneously. Committed to providing high quality programming and training, using adult teaming theory. Experienced in working with teams and individuals.

EDUCATION

University of South Carolina   Columbia, South Carolina.
Master of Education in Training and Development with a Business Management minor, May, 1992; GPA: 3.34 4.0.
Bachelor of Arts in Psychology with Counseling minor, May, 1990.

COMPETENCIES

Administration Maintained budgets for training, supplies, recognition activities, programming for summer youth programs sponsored by the City of Charleston, SC. Designed and published biweekly newsletter. Managed a 22,000 square foot facility providing a full range of recreational activities.

Advising & Counseling Advised two student organizations involving approximately 4,000 male and female students. Counseled individual students with career and personal concerns as needed. Provided on call crisis management response for 6 residence halls and 4,000 students on a rotating basis .

Facilitation Facilitated training sessions and programs for staff and students on subjects such as: total quality management, communicating with others, motivation, creativity, enthusiasm and esprit de corps, leadership, goal setting, programming, publicity, and rape and sexual assault. Facilitated diversity programs in South Carolina High Schools, 1992 and 1993. Presented programs regularly at national, regional, and state conferences. Planned, coordinated, and facilitated staff retreat for 22 paraprofessional staff members. Instructed a two credit college course, entitled Introduction to Adolescent Counseling; topics included communication, values clarification, developmental theory, diversity, and crisis management.

Recruitment Recruited counselors for summer program. Reviewed and evaluated applications and resumes. Developed improved staff selection and placement process and procedures.

Supervision Selected, trained and supervised, and evaluated staff of 22 paraprofessionals. Selected, supervised, and trained 125 Camp Counselors, and 5 Counselors in Training.

Julie M. Bartow, Page 2

<u>Training</u> Trained staff of 22 paraprofessionals in recreational projects planning. Conducted needs assessment and evaluations of on-the-job training for 185 paraprofessional staff members. Developed curriculum and packaged training materials for staff training sessions, and student programs.

SELECTED PRESENTATIONS

"Total Quality Management: Buzz Word or Bonanza," South Carolina Society of Human Resources Conference 1992.
"Stretching Dollars for Student Programs," Staff Inservice Training, Fall 1993.

HONORS

South Carolina Society of Human Resources Conference 1992 Top Program Award.
City of Charleston Certificate of Appreciation, 1993.

ACTIVITIES

American Society of Training and Development (Member, 1992-present).
Society for Human Resource Management (Chapter Program Vice President, 1991-1992).
Intramural Advisory Board (Chairperson, 1991-1992, 1992-1993).

EMPLOYMENT

Housing and Residence Life, University of South Carolina, Columbia, South Carolina, Residence Director, May 1992-present.
City of Charleston Summer Program Coordinator, May 1992-August 1993.

REFERENCES Available upon request.

ANALYSIS:

Strengths

- The individual's Summary of Qualifications acts as a Key Word Preface, highlighting her principal knowledge, skills and abilities up front where they will be seen by overworked recruiters.

- The functional layout of her resume contains a large number of key words identifying her qualifications.

- The individual's name appears on the second page of her resume so that it can be identified if separated from the first page during scanning and processing at the job bank.

Weaknesses

- The use of a functional style format makes it difficult to determine in which position she demonstrated the knowledge, skills and abilities she describes.

- The use of a box around her resume will confuse a job bank's scanner, which will read the box's vertical lines as the letter "l".

- The use of small, 10 point typeface may make it difficult for a job bank scanner to read her resume accurately.

- The use of underlining may make it difficult for a job bank's scanner to read/process the resume accurately.

- The statement regarding her References is not necessary and a waste of space on the resume.

Brian L. Simpson
1901 Near Lake Road
Huntsville, AL 35818
(205) 762 4405

OBJECTIVE:

Hands-on manager with over 10 years experience empowering high performance teams
in software engineering analysis, supporting Space Lab and other NASA technology
development programs. Seeking an opportunity in software engineering analysis that
will expand my knowledge and foster career growth.

EDUCATION:

B.S. Computer Science minor in Mathematics, University of Alabama in Huntsville,
1977
M.S. System Engineering, Thomas E. Edison Institute of Technology, (In progress)

Additional Training
Object Oriented Design and Analysis
TBE Software Engineering Course
IBM's Trusted Software Development Training
Distributed Computing Design System (DCDS) Training
Requirements Tracer (RT) Training
Technical Writing Course

EMPLOYMENT HISTORY:

IBM Aerospace Engineering, Huntsville, AL March 1990 to present
Martin Marietta, Inc., Huntsville, AL May 1980 to February 1990
Hercules Space Systems, Montgomery, AL May 1977 to May 1980

COMPETENCIES:

CASE Tools Support
- Provided managerial assistance and user support
- Coordinated developer and integration efforts with the use of DCDS and RDD

Computer Services
- Established a classified link between the IBM Research Center in Huntsville and
  the NASA Test Facility at Cape Kennedy
- Managed both classified and unclassified processing; also provided computer
  administrative support such as computer purchase requisitions, software and
  hardware installation, resource allocations, and trouble shooting

Verification and Validation
- Performed requirements analysis, requirements traceability, application of
  Trusted Software Principles, and technical document reviews
- Reviewed and prepared documentation in accordance with Military Standards
  such as MU STD 2167A

System and Software Engineering Analysis
- Identified critical issues, measures of effectiveness and parameters for defining initial requirements and simulation support
- Interfaced with government customers

PROGRAMS SUPPORTED:
BKND Software, Next Generation Software Engineering Environment, VTXTS Flight System Simulator, Lance Missile System Test Bed, SDI Early Warning Radar Systems, and Space Lab

SECURITY CLEARANCE: SECRET, PRSDI, JCSINTEL
(Department of Defense)
U.S. Citizen

ANALYSIS:

Strengths

- The resume contains a large number of technical terms and jargon likely to be used as key words by recruiters seeking to fill very specialized positions.

- The resume lists special certifications, in this case the individual's security clearances for government work on classified projects.

- On-going education and training are included, signaling a person who has a growing level of expertise in his field and a commitment to advancing his professional knowledge.

Weaknesses

- The use of a functional style format makes it difficult to determine in which position the person demonstrated the knowledge, skills and abilities he describes.

- The use of an Objective rather than a Key Word Preface forces the reviewer to search for the person's qualifications in the body of the resume.

- The use of "soft" vocabulary (e.g., "hands-on," "empowering") takes up space on the resume without adding to it key words that could be used in a computer-based search.

- The Education section should not appear in front of the Experience section, unless the person is a recent school/college graduate.

- The lack of identification on the second page of the resume could cause it to be lost if it was separated from the first page during scanning and processing at the job bank.

- The use of italics may make it difficult for a job bank's scanner to read/process the resume accurately.

A CUT ABOVE THE REST

Each year, tens of thousands of people send their resumes to Job Bank USA. Those which follow are among the best we have received. They have been carefully modified to protect the identity of the individuals whose credentials they describe. However, their key aspects—their format and content—remain largely unchanged. Consequently, they look and read much as they did when they were originally entered into the Job Bank USA computer.

These resumes stand out for one very important reason: they work. They have demonstrated both the capability and the power of an electronic resume. Indeed, these particular electronic resumes have compiled very impressive records; each has connected its owner with between five and twenty employment opportunities!

As you will see, no single resume incorporates every one of the guidelines provided in this book. All of them, however, embody the key principles of an effective electronic resume design. As a result, these resumes have been able to accomplish two critical tasks which a conventional resume simply would not be able to perform: first, they have enabled the Job Bank USA computer to recognize and understand their owners' employment credentials and second, they have matched those credentials with the qualifications that employers have specified for open jobs.

Undoubtedly, some of these matches were caused by other factors. A person's occupational field, location, salary requirement as well as the economy and time of year can and do have an impact. Nevertheless, these electronic resumes are useful models because they have a track record of success. They are not "make believe" resumes developed for a book, but actual working resumes that have met the test in the New Job Market of the 1990's. They have made electronic connections between real people and real employment opportunities. While they are not perfect, they are a cut above the rest.

Each of the following resumes is presented on a single page for ease of reference. When produced for Job Bank USA and employers using the recommended 12-14 point size, each resume would be two pages in length.

JANE SIMEON
54 Old Oak Terrace
Phoenixville, Pennsylvania 42516
Home: (215) 555-4217

QUALIFICATIONS SUMMARY:

A skilled Human Resources professional with over ten years experience in personnel functions in both a bargaining and non-bargaining setting, with much of this experience centered on employee relations.

EMPLOYMENT HISTORY:

September 1991 to May 1994: Bluebell Building Products, Philadelphia, Pennsylvania
Personnel Manager—reported to the President/CEO of a manufacturing facility with approximately 400 employees. Involved in all corporate Human Resources related functions, including recruiting and hiring; compensation management; employee benefits; pension and insurance administration; labor/employee relations; contract administration; policy formulation; workers compensation administration; and training. Major emphasis placed on management and maintenance of employee benefit costs, improvement of labor relations with the bargaining unit, and enhancement of personnel systems to improve the efficiency and overall level of support to the organization.

Significant Accomplishments:
- Successfully participated in negotiating a four year labor contract meeting corporate objectives.
- Reduced annual cost for Worker's Compensation Insurance and Group Health Plan by over 20%.
- Designed and implemented policies for Family & Medical Leave, Americans with Disabilities Act, Drug & Alcohol Abuse, and Sexual Harassment.

January 1990 to September 1991: Pennsylvania State Employees Association Philadelphia, Pennsylvania
Labor Relations Representative—reported to the Director of Employment Services of a labor organization representing over 20,000 Pennsylvania state employees. Provided assistance to state employees with job-related matters. Investigated labor problems and established facts to support grievance preparation and represented employees through all steps of the grievance procedure. Negotiated with management of state agencies to facilitate dispute resolution and grievance settlement. Attended Association meetings to advise employees of changes in state law and personnel policies.

April 1984 to December 1989: York Industries, Inc., York, Pennsylvania
Human Resources Administrator—reported to the Human Resources Division Manager of a manufacturing facility with over 2,000 employees. Directed all recruiting and hiring of shop and office bargaining employees; administered labor contracts with respect to layoff, recall and job assignments; and conducted pre-retirement interviews explaining pension benefits. In addition, served in labor relations during periods of contract negotiation and also participated in the investigation and preparation of grievances for arbitration.

EDUCATION:
Gettysburg College, Gettysburg, PA, B.S.—Business Administration, Graduated Magna Cum Laude

PROFESSIONAL ORGANIZATIONS:
National and Local Chapter Member—Society for Human Resources Management (SHRM)
Tri-State Safety Council

JOHN ST. THOMAS, CPIM
42 Apple Pine Way
Monterey, California 90708
408-886-9828

KEYWORDS

Materials and Purchasing Management. Operations Management. JIT. MRP II. TQM. DRP. Focus Forecasting. Project Management. Cost Reduction. Cycle Time Reduction. EDI. Repetitive/Custom Job Shop. Lead Time Reduction. Vender Certification Program. Sourcing & Negotiating. Barcoding. Cycle Count Program. Inventory Control. Production Planning. Master Scheduling. P&L Responsibility. CPIM Certified. BA Business—1972. LLB Law—1977.

EXPERIENCE

Independent Consultant—Central California—October, 1991 to Present
Self-employed as contract consultant for small to medium sized companies in the areas of materials, purchasing, operations and distribution.

- Several successful JIT/TQM purchasing project implementations including vender certification programs, an EDI implementation, and re-engineering for buyer/planner concept.
- Member of project team which implemented multiple distribution center DRP/focus forecasting system with extensive re-engineering of all operational systems, procedures and processes.

Atlas Generating Corp.—Salinas, CA.
Operations Manager—1990 to September 1991
Directed manufacturing, purchasing, customer service, production and master scheduling, materials planning, shipping/receiving, and facilities. 1990 sales of $8 million.

- Planned, staffed, equipped, and established a new plant start-up facility which became operational within three months from inception.
- On time shipping record; sales bookings, production rate and shipments exceeded plan by 200%.
- Reduced material costs by 10%, manufacturing labor costs by 22%, and manufacturing cycle time from 6 weeks to 4 weeks on custom products.
- Implemented a LAN based MRP II integrated manufacturing information system which was fully operational within 6 months.
- Automated the contract/project material costing and bidding process to allow 24 hour bid response to proposals.

Atlas Solar Systems Corporation—Salinas, CA
Division Materials Manager—1986 to 1990
Directed production and inventory control, purchasing, materials planning, and shipping/receiving for a multiplant manufacturer of solar power generating equipment and industrial power drives. 1990 sales of $55 million.

- Reduced subassembly stock and WIP by 35%, raw materials stock by 15%, rework by 20%, shortages by 50%.
- Member of task force which implemented a manufacturing team-centered work force, facilitating implementation of JIT and TQM concepts and techniques.
- MRP II implementation task force member.
- Instrumental in developing and implementing kanban-type material pull system for repetitive product lines, eliminating the need for kit pulls, shop orders, and Subassembly Dept.

McDonnell Douglas Corporation—1976 to 1986, St. Louis, MO.
Inventory Control and Traffic Manager for a high-technology defense systems manufacturer. Worked in all inventory, stores, receiving and shipping functions.

- Sustained inventory record accuracy of 95%.

EDUCATION

- Degree in Law from Notre Dame University—1977
- Bachelor of Business Administration from Ohio State University—1972
- APICS Certification CPIM; Working on CIRM Certification
- Extensive seminars, courses, and workshops in Logistics, JIT, Operations/Manufacturing, TQM, Plant Management, CIM, etc.
- Computer software MRP II/DRP experience on FOURTH SHIFT, MAPICS, ASK MANMAN, MCBA, and ROTH DRP/Focus Forecasting system. PC experience with Word, WordPerfect, Lotus 1-2-3, Excel.

PROFESSIONAL AFFILIATIONS

American Production and Inventory Control Society
American Management Association
National Association of Purchasing Managers

PETER OWENS THAMES
5501 Brookfield Lane
Atlanta, Georgia 30301
Home (404) 755-1245
Office (404) 873-1123

SKILLS

Administration and Management Skills: program design; zero-based budgeting; contract negotiation; planning and providing logistical and administrative support/advocacy; meeting deadlines; recruiting and training staff; supervising and evaluating staff while promoting growth and increased productivity; cost effectiveness analysis; cost benefit analysis; presenting program accomplishments; advocating program needs; proposal writing; and writing succinct reports.

Communication Skills: human relations training; small group facilitator; interpersonal processing; teaching and evaluating communications skills; establishing decision-making models; technical writing; editing; writing for publication; newsletter production; computing/word processing; multimedia utilization; platform presentation expertise; fluent Spanish; read and understand Portuguese and basic French; cross-cultural communication; establishing internal communications systems; and knowledge of computer systems, networking, architecture, hardware, software, and services concepts.

Education Skills: training needs assessment; writing training objectives; design and implementation of evaluation procedures; instructional systems design and implementation; planning and implementing comprehensive educational assessments; conducting descriptive, quasi-experimental, and evaluative research; instructional materials design; writing curricula; teaching learning theory and adapting it to real-life situations; university teaching; and workshop planning, implementation, and evaluation.

EDUCATION

Ph.D., 1983, California State University; Major: Curriculum Development and Instruction; Minors: Human Resources Development and Non-traditional Training.

B.A., 1967, Michigan State University; Major: Latin American Studies/Spanish; Minor: International Economics.

Extensive Training at IBM (1/88—10/92—ranging from "Computer Hardware, Software, Systems, and Networking" to "Project Management.")

WORK EXPERIENCE

1988—Present, IBM CORPORATION
Instructional Designer, Sales Foundation Training   Andover, MA

Provided instruction and evaluation expertise to Software Services, Networking Systems, and Hardware instructors, as well as IBM's management; developed effective communication process with 25 technical experts throughout IBM; wrote book about IBM's service products, including text and end-of-chapter tests; provided Sales Foundation Training management with research/orientation about cost effectiveness analysis and cost benefit analysis.

1968—1987 (Intermittent), CALIFORNIA STATE UNIVERSITY
Various Positions & Responsibilities   Northridge, CA

Northridge Campus Faculty and Program Manager of Hispanic Leadership Program; Instructor in Communication Skills, Learning Theory, and Media Utilization; International Education Consultant; International Rehabilitation Research Assistant; Publications Research Assistant; International Development Research Assistant.

1986, COMPETITIVE SOLUTIONS CENTER, INC.
Director of Education   Northridge, CA

Developed curricula in entrepreneurship, personal power development, and fundamentals of management. Created and standardized instructional plan and trained instructors to use same.

1983—1986, EDITING SYSTEMS, INC.
Researcher/Writer/ Editor (Self-employed)   Northridge, CA

1975—1978, U.S. DEPARTMENT OF STATE
Taipei, Taiwan—**Nonformal Education Project Coordinator**

Managed and trained a team of 22 Chinese technicians (i.e., content experts, graphic artists, photographers, and administrative personnel) to develop and implement an instructional system (i.e., needs assessment, learning objectives, instructional strategies, implementation planning, and evaluation of results) appropriate for training adults in skills and knowledge they needed. Developed and implemented communication, cost control decision-making, as well as formative and summative evaluation models allowing expeditious fulfillment of project goals.

PETER M. WILEY
Box 712
Jamestown, Virginia 22309
(804) 469-0756

PROFILE

Human Resources Generalist with over ten years experience in positions of progressive technical responsibility, including recruiting, management development and training, employee relations, benefits, compensation, HRIS, Affirmative Action Plans, and outplacement.

PROFESSIONAL BACKGROUND

03/91 to Present   MANTECH CORPORATION—Norfolk, VA
Consultant—Training Specialist for a computer science/systems integration company.
- Coordinated of all employee training, including contracting with vendors to deliver on-site training
- Designed and delivered customized training as determined by needs analysis
- Organized MANTECH Chapter of Toastmaster's International
- Reduced cost of personal computer (PC) training by 33%
- Designed database system for recording employee training records as part of ISO 9001 compliance

12/88 to 02/91   DYNAMICS RESEARCH CORPORATION—Arlington, VA
Human Resources Generalist—Site manager for a 100 employee "satellite" office completing a Pennsylvania State contract to process health insurance claims.
- Expedited recruiting and expanded low cost sources of qualified applicants
- Received certification in Zenger-Miller's "Front Line Leadership"; coordinated and facilitated training modules
- Trained supervisors and managers in DRC's employee counseling and disciplinary policies
- Introduced and administered pre-employment drug testing program
- Organized and implemented outplacement programs including Job Fairs, resume books, and interviewing workshops

04/86 to 12/88   BDM CORPORATION—McLean, VA
Human Resources Recruiter for a highly technical, 800 employee corporate headquarters and research and development facility, working on an array of government contracts.
- Successfully recruited for engineers, computer scientists, programmers and managers due to the consolidation of two offices
- Wrote interviewing manual for supervisors and managers
- Supervised integrating 300 off-site personnel records into human resource information system (HRIS)

09/85 to 04/86   SCIENCE APPLICATIONS INTERNATIONAL CORP—McLean, VA
Human Resources Administrator for a research & development facility.
- Trained three HR Administrators in all phases of Human Resources
- Conducted monthly supervisory training programs
- Introduced and organized COBRA program and 401(K) Plan
- Initiated area salary survey
- Organized employee functions
- Facilitated employee group meetings

05/84 to 09/85   GOVERNMENT EMPLOYEES INSURANCE CO.— Fairfax, VA
Assistant Manager to the V.P. of Human Resources promoted from Human Resources Coordinator—for a major auto, life, home insurance company.
- Managed high-volume recruiting (220 employees the last year)
- Initiated and conducted the first in-house training programs using AMA Supervisory Programs as well as designed additional modules
- Wrote job descriptions for all office personnel
- Implemented new HRIS
- Reestablished and improved communications in Human Resources Department and offered an innovative method to deal with employee and management problems

EDUCATION

- Graduate work at George Mason University and Marymount Universities
- B.S. from James Madison University
- Certified Facilitator—Zenger-Miller's "Front Line Leadership"
- Additional Training in Human Resources at The American University and The George Washington University as well as numerous management seminars conducted by various employers.

PROFESSIONAL ORGANIZATIONS
American Society for Training & Development
Human Resources Exchange
Society for Human Resource Management
Toastmaster's International

ETHAN L. ALBRIGHT

P.O. Box 342 Ayer, Massachusetts 01667 (508) 876-9120

OBJECTIVE

-PROJECT TECHNICAL ENGINEER / INDUSTRIAL ENGINEER-

An experienced Project/ Industrial Engineer with strong manufacturing and project management background; considerable knowledge and experience in writing technical proposals; design, development and implementation of new manufacturing systems, assembly processes, and product line introductions.

QUALIFICATIONS

PROJECT MANAGEMENT
- Staff engineer responsible for all capital equipment planning and authorizations at company level, totaling over $50M.
- Management of financial overhead/direct expense budgets and manpower planning for Production Operations Group of 300 employees and $25 million annual spend plan.
- Staff lead of Production Operations Technical Proposal efforts for claims processing equipment contracts ranging from $50-$500 million.

INDUSTRIAL ENGINEERING
- Proficient with Industrial Engineering techniques in equipment and manpower capacity modeling, inventory control systems, process flow and time study analysis, profit improvement/cost reduction programs, plant layout and material handling systems, JIT techniques, cellular manufacturing, and production simulation modeling.
- A knowledge of good manufacturing practices; process specification control and standard operating procedures in a federally regulated clean room manufacturing environment.
- Proficient computer skills: Hardware—IBM compatibles, Apple Macintosh systems, Computer Aided Design workstations. Software-Word Perfect, AutoCad, CADAM, Lotus 123, Excel, ProMod, Simfactory, Witness, Harvard Graphics & Project Mgr.

SELECTED ACHIEVEMENTS

- Project Manager of 80,000 sq. ft. facility expansion and four major new equipment/product line introductions.
- Created manufacturing process plans on CAD systems for use by assembly personnel from build to print technical drawing and data package documentation.
- Directed Industrial Engineering design, layout and implementation efforts of automated material handling production line for mail sorting units.
- Implemented and headed plant cost reduction and profit improvement program resulting in savings of four million dollars annually.

EXPERIENCE

Staff Industrial/Manufacturing Engineer   3/90 - Present
Lockheed Corporation; Patent Systems Division   Wilmington, Massachusetts
Directed a group of five engineers supporting three unique product lines. Directed Company capital equipment planning, project management and authorizations. Administered overhead and direct expenses exceeding $12 million for Product Operations group. Head of Production Operations technical business project team preparing estimates on seven multi-million dollar programs. Coordinated technical documentation of proposed material and assembly process flow, manpower staffing, equipment capacity plans, and facility layouts.

Technical Services Engineer   4/88-3/90
Raytheon Corporation   North Andover, Massachusetts
Directed the validation of primary and secondary packaging equipment in the facility, including protocol writing, equipment and process validation and product performance qualification. Fact book was also included. Led introduction of new and existing processes transferred from other facilities into North Andover facility.

Materials Management Supervisor/Production Planner 6/79-3/88
Raytheon Corporation   North Andover, Massachusetts
Administered production control, planning systems/process transfers for facility producing over 300 products. Worked on manufacturing engineering projects for operations utilizing simulation and autocad software. Supervised warehousing, shipping, receiving and duplicating operations. Led team staff of 18. Developed systems for scheduling, forecasting, procedures control and performance appraisal and compensation.

EDUCATION

Bachelor of Science, Industrial Engineering, University of Massachusetts, May 1986.
Masters in Business Administration, Boston University, May 1992.

HONORS

1992 Honorary Inductee Society of Engineers, University of Massachusetts: honorary engineering society for outstanding industrial engineering accomplishments and leadership efforts since leaving the university.

JAMES P. LINLEY
41379 Emmitsburg Road
Dayton, Ohio 47621
(513) 722-8983

SUMMARY

Senior Instructional Technologist with expertise in the areas of needs analysis, consulting, problem solving, client negotiations and training design, development and implementation for educational, federal and corporate environments.

EXPERIENCE

Pacer Training Corporation   **Dayton, OH**
Senior Instructional Technologist   1/93—Present

- Design, develop and deliver software applications training and documentation.
- Conduct needs analysis and write course design documents.
- Manage development of task deliverables and consult with clients.
- Facilitate problem solving meetings and implement solutions.
- Develop and implement formatting standards for training materials.

Ameritech Information Systems   **Chicago, IL**
Instructional Technologist   1/92—1/93

- Developed and delivered training for 400 employees in multiple locations.
- Designed facilitator guides, participant manuals and job aids.
- Revamped product training; reduced course length and increased customer satisfaction.
- Assessed employee and client training needs and developed educational plans.
- Reviewed training sections of federal proposals and made recommendations.

Junior Instructional Technologist   6/90—1/92
- Analyzed evaluation data from training courses; compiled results and generated reports.
- Designed and implemented new evaluation instrument for in-house training.
- Coordinated training for 150 employees and negotiated vendor contracts.

EDUCATION

The American University   **Washington, DC**
M.A., Instructional Systems Design   December 1990

Pennsylvania State University   **University Park, PA**
B.S., English Education and Secondary Teaching   June 1985

Northern Virginia Community College   **Alexandria, VA**
A.A.S., Liberal Arts   December 1981

Dale Carnegie Leadership Institute   **Chicago, IL**
Certificate, Effective Leadership and Public Speaking   January 1991

OTHER SKILLS

Experienced in accomplishment-based curriculum development methodology; managing multiple priorities; executive presentations and customer relations.

Ameryl P. Brown
15 Singing Bird Lane
Minneapolis, MN 56997
(612) 446-9856

CAREER SUMMARY:

An accomplished Marketing and Sales Executive with increasing management responsibility across several industries from mid-size to Fortune 100 companies. I have a strong background in package good marketing, sales, promotions and financial services. A proven record of excellence in developing and implementing successful business strategies to maximize sales and profits. I have been widely recognized for outstanding leadership skills and involvement in civic, community and professional organizations.

EDUCATION:

Southern Michigan University, BS Economics/Business, 1970
University of Michigan, MBA, Marketing and Finance, 1976

PROFESSIONAL EXPERIENCE:

Metropolitan Life Insurance Company, Minneapolis, Minnesota

1991-Present, Division Director, Long Term Products Division
Launched the first new Group Insurance product in 15 years.
Formed a new marketing division to introduce Lawyers Long Term Care Insurance.
Developed unique strategic plan to launch this new product.
Generated first year sales that achieved 300% of plan

1989-1991, Division Director, Group Insurance
Supervised the marketing unit for the second largest product group in an insurance company with $22 billion GL and LTD insurance in-force.
Reversed negative plan termination trend and generated 5% growth.
Launched award winning and campaign and all star festival that increased displays 22% and customer trails and awareness.

Shasta Beverages, Inc., Atlanta, Georgia

1987-1987, Senior Product Manager, Alternative Beverages Division, Sales $109MM
Directed Shasta's largest non-traditional consumer product group.
Developed a corporate tie-in promotion for the 1986 Stanley Cup with NHL Properties and a dozen corporations.

1980-1986, Senior Product Manager and Product Manager, Iced Teas
Developed strategic expansion programs for iced teas. Achieved company's highest annual sales and market share in this category by:
  Creating first national consumer promotion
  Creating three linked commercials to increase interest, awareness and trial.
  Developing a modular display program that achieved the beverage's highest share of retail displays and inventory (23% and 45%).
  Growing market share 12% with greater ads and display support.
  Introducing decaffeinated version of iced teas, resulting in 15% sales increase.
  Cutting production cost by $4MM with IMA packaging project.
  Developing new packing graphics for entire product line.

NATIONAL CONTAINER CORPORATION, CHICAGO, ILLINOIS

1978-1980, Assistant Product Manager, Retail Packaging, Sales $55MM
Reversed declining sales trends and achieved 15% market share with new modular design introduction.
Conducted market analysis (SAM, A.C. Nielsen, Majers)
Developed and evaluated consumer and trade promotions.

1975-1977, Area Manager, Chicago
Supervised sales representatives, increased shipping package sales by 32% and display stand sales by 25% through monthly sales training seminars.
Secured National Container's first combined product introduction (valued at $300MM) at Stop ^ Shop Stores, the company's largest account.

1970-1975, Retail Sales Representative, Chicago
Consistently exceeded sales quota and won numerous sales contests.

PERSONAL:
University of Michigan, School of Business Board of Advisors, since 1991.
Selected "Outstanding Young Men of America," 1975 and 1982.
Honored for Outstanding Leadership and Contributions to the Business Community by University of Minnesota, 1990.

Albert J. Black
5216 Jayhawk Street
Seattle, Washington 98922
(206) 497-2094

CURRENT POSITION:

Project Manager for Curriculum Development with the Community Services and Continuing Education Division, Seattle Community College, Seattle, Washington (August 1989 to present)

Duties include managing the Curriculum Development Project, estimate project costs, monitor projects for quality and cost, supervise instructional designers, complete special projects for Dean of Division and Department Directors. Hire instructional designers.

EXPERIENCE/SKILLS:

HEAD INSTRUCTIONAL DESIGNER with Professional Studies Institute, Seattle Community College, Seattle, Washington: Supervise instructional designers and subject matter experts and coordinate the design and development of instructional materials. Conduct needs analyses and assessments; evaluate training and training materials. Consult with internal and external clients including business, industry, government, and educational institutions. Initiate and facilitate cross functional teams toward solving identified needs and effecting change. Educate and develop internal staff and external clients in the application of systematic instructional design. (August 1989 to July 1991)

TRAINING COORDINATOR with Microsoft, Inc. in Spokane, Washington: Managed training function in facility of 2,000 employees. Coordinated development of facility-wide training program, conducted needs assessments, evaluated program effectiveness, and instructed management personnel in training methods and techniques. Performed training specialist responsibilities. (April 1988 to July 1989)

TRAINING SPECIALIST (temporary) with Microsoft, Inc. (Became regular employee 07/01/85): Planned, produced, directed, and evaluated training programs and materials using skills and knowledge in problem definition, needs assessment, writing, editing, graphics, photographic, and videographic techniques; assigned and monitored training and documentation of training; formulated training policies, using knowledge of identified training needs, company production processes, and business systems; conferred with and assisted supervisors and managers in delivering training.

ASSISTANT EDITOR with the Institute for Educational Studies, Washington State University: Edited research manuscripts and supervised production; wrote articles for two periodic newsletters; designed publications lists and catalogs. (1980 to 1985)

RESOURCE INFORMATION SPECIALIST/EDITOR with Department of Agricultural Development, Washington State University: Wrote, edited, and supervised production of a regional, monthly newsletter on agriculture and natural resource issues. This four-color, offset-printed digest provided a missing news link for over 1,000 professional and citizen groups in the Northwest. (1977 to 1980)
MEMBER: American Society for Training and Development
National Society for Performance and Instruction

EDUCATION:

- Master of Arts, Adult and Continuing Education, Cornell University. (1991)
- Course work in Media Technology Program, Spokane Community College. (1986 to 1988)
- Course work in Commercial Art Program, Spokane Community College. (1980 to 1986)
- Bachelor of Science, Washington State University, Department of Agricultural Development. Curriculum included a cluster of courses in written, spoken, and visual communications. Other courses included land and water management, land economics and the like. (1977)

JAMES P. SIMMONS

8901 Abbott Street
Dallas, Texas 47711

(214) 446-8964

PROFESSIONAL SUMMARY

Analytical and detailed-oriented professional with over 16 years of experience in MIS, five years of materials management experience, seven years of experience in the marketing/sales of computer equipment, combined with extensive academic and training credentials.

AREAS OF EXPERTISE

Computer Operations   Materials Management
Systems Installation   Production Control Management
Account Management   Computer Security
Inventory Control   Budget Preparation
Forecasting & Scheduling

PROFESSIONAL HISTORY

E-SYSTEMS, INCORPORATED
Director, Management Information Systems, Dallas, Texas 1990-1994
Tasks and responsibilities included planning and installation of a MRP System, two Local Area Networks (LANs), an Electronic Data Interchange (EDI) and all software/hardware upgrades; establishment of computer security and disaster recovery procedures; technical staff supervision and software application analysis; software/hardware cost analysis; and contract negotiations with vendors and consulting for major strategic business unit.
- Reduced operating costs by 12% over a three-year period.
- Negotiated a five-year service agreement, saving $58,000 a year.
- Directed the conversion from MAI/Basic 4 to IBM AS/400 three months ahead of schedule, saving $29,000 in maintenance costs.

Director of Materials, Dallas, Texas 1990
Managed materials for the Software Systems Division, with responsibility for inventory levels, purchasing, production control, progress posting, forecasting, transportation and scheduling.
- Increased on-time customer shipments by 10%.
- Reduced inventory stocks by 14%.

IBM CORPORATION, Arlington, TX 1983-1990
Senior Account Representative
Sold software applications and hardware; managed accounts; forecasted sales; marketed computer solutions such as MRP Systems, Shop Floor Control, Bar Code Systems and CAD/CAM to manufacturers; and prepared contracts.
- Achieved over $22,000,000 in sales of goods and services.
- Company Achievement Award (1984).
- District Sales Champ (1983).

DELL COMPUTER CORPORATION, Austin, TX 1981-1983
Shop Floor Control Supervisor
Directed the master production schedule and shop scheduling; material movements in three shops; inventory control; and labor assignments in the Manufacturing Group.
- Increased the number of on-time customer shipments.

TEXAS INSTRUMENTS
Superintendent of Process Control, Dallas, TX 1978-1981
Managed the Master Production Schedule as well as material movements between five shops; progress posting; and shipping and manpower forecasts and utilization.
- Reduced shop lead times.
- Increased manpower productivity via improved movement of materials.

General Manager-Office Computer Operations, Dallas, TX 1973-1978
Managed computer security, system upgrades and maintenance across five computer facilities with 75 personnel; developed disaster recovery procedures; and negotiated contracts with vendors.
- Reduced overtime 50% by introducing a three-day work week of 36 hours for computer operators.

ACADEMIC & PROFESSIONAL CREDENTIALS

Bachelor of Business Administration
Major: Computer Science; Minor: Accounting
University of Texas; Arlington, Texas
American Production & Inventory Control Society (APICS)
CPIM Certification

10

15 STEPS TO A HIGH POWERED ELECTRONIC RESUME

*T*he following 15 steps present a systematic, organized approach that will enable you to write your own high powered electronic resume. This process will not eliminate the thought, the energy or the time commitment required to develop any good resume, conventional or electronic. It does, however, give you the framework and direction you need to create an effective resume without wasting time, without a lot of frustration, and without the expense involved in having someone else write your resume. Follow this step-by-step process carefully, and you will produce your own electronic resume with the "right stuff"—the right format and substance to plug you into the New Job Market and connect you with the great job opportunities it offers.

Before you begin, however, take a moment to review the following important principles and procedures. They are the bedrock of the process, so you must understand and adhere to them for the process to work for you.

1. **Give your resume the attention it deserves.** Find a quiet room and enough time that you can get some concentrated work done. The step-wise process I've provided here will enable you to stop that effort at logical "break points," so that you can do something else (if you must) and then return to your work on your resume later.

2. **This is not a test.** In fact, I've included a reference note for you, in each of the steps. This note will direct you back to the discussion, earlier in the book, of the particular aspect of resume writing each step involves. The references are there to help you understand the rationale and mechanics of each step and to assist you in completing it. So, don't rely on your memory; use the references as you work through the steps. You'll produce a better resume, as a result.

3. **You're doing something new and different.** You're developing a special kind of resume, an electronic resume. Don't mix the advice and counsel of relatives, friends, business associates or even professional resume writers, however well intentioned, in this process. Their background and frame of reference is almost certainly the conventional resume, and mixing that document with an electronic resume will yield a confusing and ineffective jumble of styles and techniques.

If you'll keep these guidelines in mind and follow the steps below, you'll have everything you need to develop the most advanced and the most powerful resume available anywhere today—your own electronic resume.

DEVELOP THE KEY WORD PREFACE

Step 1
Determine the Selection Criteria for the Job You Want
Refer to pages 54 and 55

List below the critical qualifications for the specific position or category of positions you are seeking in your job search. Add to the list any other skills or experience that could enhance a person's performance on-the-job. These credentials are the selection criteria for the position you want. Your resume should be tightly focused on them. The following documents and resources will help you to identify these criteria: the position description for the new job, recruitment ads for the position or similar positions in your industry, the insights of other individuals who have held the position successfully in the past, headhunters or executive recruiters specializing in your field, and your own professional, technical or trade association.

_____   _____
_____   _____
_____   _____
_____   _____
_____   _____
_____   _____
_____   _____
_____   _____
_____   _____
_____   _____
_____   _____
_____   _____
_____   _____

Step 2
Identify the Key Words for Your Electronic Resume
Refer to pages 55 through 58

Identify up to 10 key words to describe each of your **ASSETS**. Record these words in the spaces provided in the first column below. The following documents and resources will help you to determine the nouns and phrases which best apply to you: any previous resumes that you've written, position descriptions for your current and/or past positions, performance evaluation reports from your current and/or past supervisors, the results of any skills or interest inventory assessment and the learning objectives for any education or training program you've attended in the past five years.

ABILITIES

Key Word	Synonym	Value
_____	_____	___
_____	_____	___
_____	_____	___

_____	_____	_____
_____	_____	_____
_____	_____	_____
_____	_____	_____
_____	_____	_____
_____	_____	_____
_____	_____	_____
_____	_____	_____
_____	_____	_____
_____	_____	_____
_____	_____	_____
_____	_____	_____

SPECIAL AWARDS & RECOGNITION

Key Words	Synonyms	Value
_____	_____	_____
_____	_____	_____
_____	_____	_____
_____	_____	_____
_____	_____	_____
_____	_____	_____
_____	_____	_____
_____	_____	_____
_____	_____	_____
_____	_____	_____

SPECIAL LICENSES & CERTIFICATIONS

Key Words	Synonyms	Value
_____	_____	_____
_____	_____	_____
_____	_____	_____
_____	_____	_____
_____	_____	_____
_____	_____	_____
_____	_____	_____
_____	_____	_____

_____   _____   _____
_____   _____   _____

EXPERIENCE

Key Words	Synonyms	Value
_____	_____	____
_____	_____	____
_____	_____	____
_____	_____	____
_____	_____	____
_____	_____	____
_____	_____	____
_____	_____	____
_____	_____	____
_____	_____	____
_____	_____	____
_____	_____	____
_____	_____	____
_____	_____	____

TRAINING

Key Words	Synonyms	Value
_____	_____	____
_____	_____	____
_____	_____	____
_____	_____	____
_____	_____	____
_____	_____	____
_____	_____	____
_____	_____	____
_____	_____	____

Using the spaces provided in the second column above, note the principal **SYNONYMS** in your field for as many of your key words as possible. These **SYNONYMS** are nouns or phrases that have the same meaning or a similar meaning to the key words you've listed for each **ASSET**. However, this step is not a dictionary exercise. In other words, you should **include only those synonyms that are used interchangeably in your field with the key words that describe your ASSETS.**

Step 3
Determine the Importance of Each Key Word in Your ASSETS
Refer to pages 54 through 58

Using the selection criteria you developed in Step 1, evaluate the importance of the key words in each of your **ASSETS** and rank order them. Assign a value of 10 to the most important and the value of 1 to the least important qualification you have among each of your **ASSETS.** The goal here is for you to designate the value an employer would use in evaluating prospective candidates for the job you want, rather than your personal judgment of its importance. Enter each asset's ranking in the space provided in the "Value" column above.

Step 4
Develop Your Key Word Preface
Refer to pages 58 and 59

The Key Word Preface is limited to 25 or 30 nouns or phrases that describe your most important **ASSETS** for the job you want. Therefore, using the rank ordering you assigned in Step 3, select the top five or six key words in each of your **ASSETS** and enter them in the spaces below. Remember, the first letter of each word is capitalized, except for "and," "or," "the," and other connector words. Each key word or phrase is followed by a period.

_____. _____. _____.
_____. _____. _____.
_____. _____. _____.
_____. _____. _____.
_____. _____. _____.
_____. _____. _____.
_____. _____. _____.
_____. _____. _____.
_____. _____. _____.

DEVELOP THE EXPERIENCE SECTION OF YOUR ELECTRONIC RESUME

Step 5
Document Your Employment History
Refer to pages 59 through 61

List all of your employers in reverse chronological order (i.e., the most recent first) and the dates of your employment. Each employer's name should be presented in all capital letters. State the month and year of each date as follows: 5/93—6/94.

Employer's Name   Dates of Employment

_____   _____

_____   _____

_____   _____

_____   _____

_____   _____

_____   _____

_____   _____

_____   _____

_____   _____

_____   _____

_____   _____

_____   _____

_____   _____

Step 6
Identify the Positions You Held While Working for Each Employer
Refer to pages 59 through 61

For each employer listed in Step 5 above, list the position or positions you held in reverse chronological order. Each position title should appear in initial capital letters (i.e., the first letter of all nouns is capitalized). Also state the month and year you held each position using the same format you used in Step 5.

Employer: _____   Dates: _____
Position(s):   Dates:

_____   _____
_____   _____
_____   _____
_____   _____
_____   _____

Employer: _____   Dates: _____
Position(s):   Dates:

_____   _____
_____   _____
_____   _____
_____   _____
_____   _____

Employer: _____   Dates: _____
Position(s):   Dates:

_____   _____
_____   _____
_____   _____
_____   _____
_____   _____

Employer: _____   Dates: _____
Position(s):   Dates:

_____   _____
_____   _____
_____   _____
_____   _____

Employer: _____   Dates: _____
Position(s):   Dates:

_____   _____
_____   _____

_____   _____

_____   _____

_____   _____

Employer: _____   Dates: _____

Position(s):   Dates:

_____   _____

_____   _____

_____   _____

_____   _____

_____   _____

Employer: _____   Dates: _____

Position(s):   Dates:

_____   _____

_____   _____

_____   _____

_____   _____

_____   _____

Employer: _____   Dates: _____

Position(s):   Dates:

_____   _____

_____   _____

_____   _____

_____   _____

_____   _____

Employer: _____   Dates: _____

Position(s):   Dates:

_____   _____

_____   _____

_____   _____

_____   _____

_____   _____

Employer: _____   Dates: _____

Position(s):   Dates:

_____   _____

_____   _____
_____   _____
_____   _____
_____   _____

Employer: _____   Dates: _____
Position(s):   Dates:

_____   _____
_____   _____
_____   _____
_____   _____
_____   _____

Employer: _____   Dates: _____
Position(s):   Dates:

_____   _____
_____   _____
_____   _____
_____   _____
_____   _____

Employer: _____   Dates: _____
Position(s):   Dates:

_____   _____
_____   _____
_____   _____
_____   _____
_____   _____

Step 7
Identify the Knowledge, Skills & Abilities You Used On-the-Job
Refer to pages 61 through 64

For each of the positions that you identified in Step 6, use the key words you developed in Step 2 to list those qualifications and capabilities that you demonstrated in the position. These key words should identify all of the knowledge, skills and abilities you used to accomplish the tasks and activities for which you were responsible. You may include the same key word(s) in more than one position, but you should use all of the key words at least once.

Wherever possible, use the synonyms of a key word, once the key word itself has been used in the Key Word Preface or for another position.

Employer: _____   Dates:_____
Position: _____ Dates:

_____   _____

Key words:

_____. _____. _____.
_____. _____. _____.
_____. _____. _____.
_____. _____. _____.
_____. _____. _____.

Employer: _____   Dates:_____
Position: _____ Dates:

_____   _____

Key words:

_____. _____. _____.
_____. _____. _____.
_____. _____. _____.
_____. _____. _____.
_____. _____. _____.

Employer: _____   Dates:_____
Position: _____ Dates:

_____   _____

Key words:

_____. _____. _____.
_____. _____. _____.
_____. _____. _____.
_____. _____. _____.
_____. _____. _____.

Employer: _____   Dates:_____
Position: _____ Dates:

_____   _____

Key words:

_____. _____. _____.
_____. _____. _____.

_____. _____. _____.
_____. _____. _____.
_____. _____. _____.

Employer: _____   Dates:_____
Position: Dates:
_____   _____

Key words:

_____. _____. _____.
_____. _____. _____.
_____. _____. _____.
_____. _____. _____.
_____. _____. _____.

Employer: _____   Dates:_____
Position: Dates:
_____   _____

Key words:

_____. _____. _____.
_____. _____. _____.
_____. _____. _____.
_____. _____. _____.
_____. _____. _____.

Employer: _____   Dates:_____
Position: Dates:
_____   _____

Key words:

_____. _____. _____.
_____. _____. _____.
_____. _____. _____.
_____. _____. _____.
_____. _____. _____.

Employer: _____   Dates:_____
Position: Dates:
_____   _____

Key words:

_____. _____. _____.

_____. _____. _____.
_____. _____. _____.
_____. _____. _____.
_____. _____. _____.

Employer: _____ Dates:_____
Position: Dates:
_____ _____

Key words:

_____. _____. _____.
_____. _____. _____.
_____. _____. _____.
_____. _____. _____.
_____. _____. _____.

Employer: _____ Dates:_____
Position: Dates:
_____ _____

Key words:

_____. _____. _____.
_____. _____. _____.
_____. _____. _____.
_____. _____. _____.
_____. _____. _____.

Employer: _____ Dates:_____
Position: Dates:
_____ _____

Key words:

_____. _____. _____.
_____. _____. _____.
_____. _____. _____.
_____. _____. _____.
_____. _____. _____.

Employer: _____ Dates:_____
Position: Dates:
_____ _____

Key words:

_____. _____. _____.
_____. _____. _____.
_____. _____. _____.
_____. _____. _____.
_____. _____. _____.

Employer: _____   Dates:_____
Position: Dates:
_____ _____

Key words:

_____. _____. _____.
_____. _____. _____.
_____. _____. _____.
_____. _____. _____.
_____. _____. _____.

Employer: _____   Dates:_____
Position: Dates:
_____ _____

Key words:

_____. _____. _____.
_____. _____. _____.
_____. _____. _____.
_____. _____. _____.
_____. _____. _____.

Employer: _____   Dates:_____
Position: Dates:
_____ _____

Key words:

_____. _____. _____.
_____. _____. _____.
_____. _____. _____.
_____. _____. _____.
_____. _____. _____.

Employer: _____   Dates:_____
Position: _____   Dates:

_____   _____

Key words:

_____. _____. _____.
_____. _____. _____.
_____. _____. _____.
_____. _____. _____.
_____. _____. _____.

Employer: _____   Dates:_____
Position: _____   Dates:

_____   _____

Key words:

_____. _____. _____.
_____. _____. _____.
_____. _____. _____.
_____. _____. _____.
_____. _____. _____.

Employer: _____   Dates:_____
Position: _____   Dates:

_____   _____

Key words:

_____. _____. _____.
_____. _____. _____.
_____. _____. _____.
_____. _____. _____.
_____. _____. _____.

Employer: _____   Dates:_____
Position: _____   Dates:

_____   _____

Key words:

_____. _____. _____.
_____. _____. _____.
_____. _____. _____.
_____. _____. _____.
_____. _____. _____.

Employer: _____   Dates:_____

Position: _____   Dates:

                          _____

Key words:

_____. _____. _____.

_____. _____. _____.

_____. _____. _____.

_____. _____. _____.

_____. _____. _____.

Employer: _____   Dates:_____

Position: _____   Dates:

                          _____

Key words:

_____. _____. _____.

_____. _____. _____.

_____. _____. _____.

_____. _____. _____.

_____. _____. _____.

Employer: _____   Dates:_____

Position: _____   Dates:

                          _____

Key words:

_____. _____. _____.

_____. _____. _____.

_____. _____. _____.

_____. _____. _____.

_____. _____. _____.

Step 8
Document Your Experience in Each Position
Refer ot pages 61 through 64

Using the key words for each position that you listed in Step 7, develop three-to-five sentences which describe what you did with those key words on-the-job. Do not use "responsibility sentences" (i.e., I was responsible for this." "I was responsible for that."). Instead, write sentences that have three elements: the key word + a statement of what you did with them + some benefit achieved by those actions.

Employer: _____   Dates:_____
Position: _____   Dates: _____

Key Word Sentences:
_____
_____
_____
_____
_____
_____
_____

Employer: _____   Dates:_____
Position: _____   Dates: _____

Key Word Sentences:
_____
_____
_____
_____
_____
_____
_____

Employer: _____   Dates:_____
Position: _____   Dates: _____

Key Word Sentences:
_____
_____
_____
_____
_____
_____

Employer: _____   Dates:_____
Position: Dates:

_____   _____

Key Word Sentences:

_____

_____

_____

_____

_____

_____

_____

Employer: _____   Dates:_____
Position: Dates:

_____   _____

Key Word Sentences:

_____

_____

_____

_____

_____

_____

_____

Employer: _____   Dates:_____
Position: Dates:

_____   _____

Key Word Sentences:

_____

_____

_____

_____

_____

_____

Employer: _____   Dates:_____
Position: Dates:

_____   _____

Key Word Sentences:

_____
_____
_____
_____
_____
_____
_____

Employer: _____   Dates:_____
Position: Dates:
_____   _____

Key Word Sentences:

_____
_____
_____
_____
_____
_____
_____

Employer: _____   Dates:_____
Position: Dates:
_____   _____

Key Word Sentences:

_____
_____
_____
_____
_____
_____
_____

Employer: _____   Dates:_____
Position: Dates:
_____   _____

Key Word Sentences:

_____
_____

_____

_____

_____

_____

_____

Employer: _____   Dates:_____
Position: Dates:
_____   _____

Key Word Sentences:

_____

_____

_____

_____

_____

_____

_____

Employer: _____   Dates:_____
Position: Dates:
_____   _____

Key Word Sentences:

_____

_____

_____

_____

_____

_____

_____

Employer: _____   Dates:_____
Position: Dates:
_____   _____

Key Word Sentences:

_____

_____

_____

_____

_____

_____

_____

Employer: _____   Dates:_____
Position: Dates:

_____

Key Word Sentences:

_____

_____

_____

_____

_____

_____

_____

Employer: _____   Dates:_____
Position: Dates:

_____

Key Word Sentences:

_____

_____

_____

_____

_____

_____

_____

Employer: _____   Dates:_____
Position: Dates:

_____

Key Word Sentences:

_____

_____

_____

_____

_____

_____

_____

Employer: _____   Dates:_____
Position: Dates:

_____   _____

Key Word Sentences:

_____
_____
_____
_____
_____
_____
_____

Employer: _____   Dates:_____
Position: Dates:

_____   _____

Key Word Sentences:

_____
_____
_____
_____
_____
_____
_____

Employer: _____   Dates:_____
Position: Dates:

_____   _____

Key Word Sentences:

_____
_____
_____
_____
_____
_____
_____

Employer: _____   Dates:_____
Position: Dates:

_____   _____

Key Word Sentences:

_____

_____

_____

_____

_____

_____

_____

Employer: _____   Dates:_____
Position: Dates:

_____   _____

Key Word Sentences:

_____

_____

_____

_____

_____

_____

_____

Employer: _____   Dates:_____
Position: Dates:

_____   _____

Key Word Sentences:

_____

_____

_____

_____

_____

_____

_____

Employer: _____   Dates:_____
Position: Dates:

_____   _____

Key Word Sentences:

_____

_____

_____

_____

_____

_____

_____

Step 9
Document Your Accomplishments On-the-Job
Refer to pages 64 through 66

Identify one-to-three accomplishments that you achieved in each of the positions you've held. Wherever possible, these statements should include quantitative measures of the benefit or value of the accomplishment (e.g., "Improved sales 20% in just 6 months.").

Employer: _____   Dates:_____
Position: Dates:

_____   _____

Accomplishments:

_____

_____

_____

_____

Employer: _____   Dates:_____
Position: Dates:

_____   _____

Accomplishments:

_____

_____

_____

_____

Employer: _____   Dates:_____
Position: Dates:

_____   _____

Accomplishments:

_____

_____

_____

_____

Employer: _____   Dates:_____
Position: Dates:

_____   _____

Accomplishments:

_____

_____

_____

_____

Employer: _____   Dates:_____
Position: Dates:

_____   _____

Accomplishments:

_____

_____

_____

_____

Employer: _____   Dates:_____
Position: Dates:

_____   _____

Accomplishments:

_____

_____

_____

_____

Employer: _____   Dates:_____
Position: Dates:

_____   _____

Accomplishments:

_____

_____

_____

_____

Employer: _____   Dates:_____

Position: _____   Dates:

_____   _____

Accomplishments:

_____

_____

_____

_____

Employer: _____   Dates:_____

Position: _____   Dates:

_____   _____

Accomplishments:

_____

_____

_____

_____

Employer: _____   Dates:_____

Position: _____   Dates:

_____   _____

Accomplishments:

_____

_____

_____

_____

Employer: _____   Dates:_____

Position: _____   Dates:

_____   _____

Accomplishments:

_____

_____

_____

_____

Employer: _____   Dates:_____

Position: _____   Dates:

_____   _____

Accomplishments:

_____

_____

_____

_____

Employer: _____   Dates:_____
Position: Dates:

_____   _____

Accomplishments:

_____

_____

_____

_____

Employer: _____   Dates:_____
Position: Dates:

_____   _____

Accomplishments:

_____

_____

_____

_____

Employer: _____   Dates:_____
Position: Dates:

_____   _____

Accomplishments:

_____

_____

_____

_____

Employer: _____   Dates:_____
Position: Dates:

_____   _____

Accomplishments:

_____

_____

_____

_____

Employer: _____   Dates:_____
Position: Dates:
_____   _____

Accomplishments:

_____

_____

_____

_____

Employer: _____   Dates:_____
Position: Dates:
_____   _____

Accomplishments:

_____

_____

_____

_____

Employer: _____   Dates:_____
Position: Dates:
_____   _____

Accomplishments:

_____

_____

_____

_____

Employer: _____   Dates:_____
Position: Dates:
_____   _____

Accomplishments:

_____

_____

_____

_____

DEVELOP THE EDUCATION SECTION OF YOUR ELECTRONIC RESUME

Step 10
Identify Your Formal Education
Refer to pages 66 through 68

List all of the formal degrees, certificates and/or diplomas you have received, in reverse chronological order. Next to each degree/certificate/ diploma, identify the institution from which you received the degree/certificate/ diploma and the date it was awarded. If you included the degree or certificate in your Key Word Preface, include it again here using a synonym or widely recognized abbreviation. Do **not**, however, use an acronym for your degree/ certificate/diploma in the Education section.

Degree/Certificate/Diploma   Institution   Date

_____

_____

_____

_____

_____

_____

_____

_____

_____

Step 11
Document Your Continuing Education & Training
Refer to pages 68 and 69

List any continuing education or training program you have attended in the last five years. Identify the subject or title of the course first, then the institution where you took it (or are taking it) and the date you completed it (or state "On-going" if you're still taking the course). Use key words from the list you developed in Step 2, wherever possible.

Course Title/Subject   Institution   Date

_____

_____

_____

_____

_____

_____

_____

_____

Step 12
Document Your Licenses & Certifications
Refer to pages 69 and 70

List any licenses or formal certifications you have earned. Identify the formal name of the license, using key words from your list in Step 2, if possible; the institution or agency which awarded it; any identifying number or code which designates your particular license/certification or assigns it to you; and the date it was awarded or most recently renewed.

License/Certification   Agency/Organization   Identifying Number/Code   Date

_____

_____

_____

_____

_____

_____

_____

_____

DEVELOP THE PROFESSIONAL AFFILIATIONS & AWARDS SECTION OF YOUR ELECTRONIC RESUME

Step 13
Document Your Activities and Achievements in
Your Professional or Trade Association
Refer to pages 70 through 73

List the professional, technical and trade associations or societies to which you belong. Identify any position you've held with these organizations and any major activity or task you've performed on its behalf (e.g., Conference

Chairman, paper presentation) and the corresponding date for your involvement. Wherever possible, use key words from your list in Step 2.

Association/Society/Trade Organization   Position/Activity   Date

_____

_____

_____

_____

_____

_____

_____

_____

Step 14
Document Your Other Professional Activities & Accomplishments
Refer to pages 70 through 71

Identify any other activity or event in which you were involved that demonstrates your commitment to and on-going development in your field of expertise. List the organization or group which sponsored or supported your activity and then the activity itself, as well as the year in which it occurred.

Organization/Group   Activity/Event   Date

_____

_____

_____

_____

_____

_____

_____

CREATE YOUR OWN HIGH
POWERED ELECTRONIC RESUME

Step 15
Build Your Electronic Resume by Compiling
the Results of Steps 1-14 Above
Refer to pages 40 through 73

Compile the substance of your occupational credentials into the format prescribed for an electronic resume. Then, input the document into a word processor and print it out with a laser printer or have it produced at a local copy shop. Use white paper and black ink to ensure its compatibility with the computer-based technology of job banks.

Your Name
Street Address
City/State
Contact Telephone

KEY WORD PREFACE:

_____. _____. _____.
_____. _____. _____.
_____. _____. _____.
_____. _____. _____.
_____. _____. _____.
_____. _____. _____.
_____. _____. _____.
_____. _____. _____.

EXPERIENCE:

MOST RECENT EMPLOYER:_____Dates: _____
Most Recent Position: _____Dates: _____
Key Word Sentences:

_____
_____
_____
_____

Accomplishments:

-
-
-

Previous Position: _____Dates: _____
Key Word Sentences:

_____
_____
_____
_____

Accomplishments:

-
-
-

Previous Position: _____Dates: _____
Key Word Sentences:

_____
_____
_____
_____

Accomplishments:

-
-
-

Previous Position: _____Dates: _____
Key Word Sentences:

_____
_____
_____
_____

Accomplishments:

-
-
-

PREVIOUS EMPLOYER: _____ Dates: _____
Most Recent Position: _____Dates: _____
Key Word Sentences:

_____

_____

_____

_____

Accomplishments:

-
-
-

Previous Position: _____Dates: _____
Key Word Sentences:

_____

_____

_____

_____

Accomplishments:

-
-
-

Previous Position: _____ Dates: _____
Key Word Sentences:

_____

_____

_____

_____

Accomplishments:

■

■

■

Previous Position: _____Dates: _____
Key Word Sentences:

_____

_____

_____

_____

Accomplishments:

■

■

■

PREVIOUS EMPLOYER: _____ Dates: _____
Most Recent Position: _____Dates: _____
Key Word Sentences:

_____

_____

_____

_____

Accomplishments:

■

■

■

Previous Position: _____Dates: _____
Key Word Sentences:

_____

_____

_____

_____

Accomplishments:

■

■

■

Previous Position: _____Dates: _____

Key Word Sentences:

_____

_____

_____

_____

Accomplishments:

■

■

■

Previous Position: _____Dates: _____

Key Word Sentences:

_____

_____

_____

_____

Accomplishments:

■

■

■

EDUCATION:

Degree/Certificate/Diploma	Institution	Date

Course Title/Subject	Institution	Date

License/Certification	Agency/Organization	Identifying Number/Code	Date

PROFESSIONAL AFFILIATIONS & AWARDS:

Association/Society/Trade Organization	Position/Activity	Date

Organization/Group	Activity/Event	Date

JOB BANK EVALUATION
AND MEMBERSHIP RESOURCES

THE JOB BANK EVALUATION QUESTIONNAIRE

Use the questionnaire on page 140 to evaluate commercial job banks as well as those provided by associations, alumni groups and other organizations. The survey is not fail safe, but it will provide you with a number of important insights about the stability, performance and credibility of a prospective job bank, **before** you pay a fee for its services.

Questions	Job Bank USA	Job Bank #2	Job Bank #3	Job Bank #4
1. How long in business?	7+ yrs.			
2. How many employers use it?	700+[1]			
3. How many searches in past year? (ratio of searches/people enrolled)	1/22[2]			
4. How many people in job bank?	20,000+[1]			
5. How many people matched in past year?	55.4%[2]			
6. How many people interviewed by employer to which referred?	62%[2]			
7. Updates/modifications to resume permitted?	YES; free			
8. What information provided to employer?	photostat of original resume			
9. What safeguards are used to protect confidentiality?	Telephone call for approval prior to referral			
10. What organizations endorse or support the job bank?	250+ associations, alumni and trade groups			

[1]As of May, 1994
[2]For January-December, 1993

JOB BANK USA INFORMATION AND ENROLLMENT MATERIALS

The following pages will tell you more about the capabilities and services of Job Bank USA. While admitting to some bias, I think you'll find that Job Bank USA is an extraordinary resource with genuine value in the New Job Market. It can help plug you into the employment opportunities in that market and provide you with the knowledge, skills and information you need to manage your career successfully. Call it a form of "career insurance" for the employment hyperspace of the 1990's. It's something you can count on, year-in and year-out to help you move forward toward your career goals.

This book will ensure that you develop the kind of resume—**an electronic resume**—that will enable you to take full advantage of Job Bank USA's benefits. In addition, as my way of saying thank you for purchasing this book, I am pleased to provide the coupon below for a $10.00 discount on the normal enrollment fee for Job Bank USA. Just attach the coupon to your enrollment materials and subtract $10.00 from the annual enrollment fee of $125.00.

As a result, **you** can enroll in Job Bank USA for a full year for only $115.00, or less than $2.50 a week. That's a small and very smart investment to make in the future of your career!

DISCOUNT COUPON

This coupon entitles the bearer to a discount of $10.00 on a one year membership in Job Bank USA.

Ten and--- *no/100 Dollars*
No Photocopies

memo *Thanks for buying my book*   *Peter D. Weddle*

JOB BANK USA
Career Advancement Service

Millions of new jobs are being created in the U.S. every year. Many of these positions offer work that is interesting and filled with challenge. They have great advancement potential and provide outstanding compensation and rewards.

Yet, one in five Americans-25 million people-were out of work at one time or another in the past year. Some were able to find a new position right away. Many others, however, were forced to work part time or to accept jobs below their skill level.

It's a shocking, even frightening situation. How do you survive in such an environment? How do you keep your career on track? How do you avoid the pitfalls and capture the opportunities in today's ever changing workplace?

In the past, most people have counted on their employers to take care of them. In the 1990's, however, you can't rely on that kind of support. Companies are under siege from foreign competition. Government budgets are shrinking rapidly. Everywhere, everyone is trying to do more with less.

In this environment, your employer just can't take care of you. Instead, you must take care of yourself. Whether you're a salesman or an engineer, a plant worker or an executive, from now on you're going to have to manage your own career. And **JOB BANK USA** offers a Career Advancement Service to help you do just that.

JOB BANK USA
The Right Stuff for the 1990's!

JOB BANK USA is the state-of-the-art employment services company in the USA. Its computerized Career Advancement Service gives you two important benefits: **Electronic Networking** to some of the best open positions nationwide and a personal **Career Tool Kit** to help you manage your career successfully.

Electronic Networking

There are lots of employment opportunities in the USA, but the question is, "How do you find them?" Most of the open positions in the job market are never advertised. In fact, some authorities estimate that this "Hidden Job Market" now includes as many as two-thirds of all available jobs. And experience has shown that the best way to tap the Hidden Job Market is by **networking**, by connecting with the right employer with the right job at the right time.

Now, you can use the power of advanced technology to extend the reach and the effectiveness of your networking. **JOB BANK USA**'s unique Electronic Networking system enables you to connect with employment opportunities 24 hours a day, 7 days a week. You can network while you're sleeping, while you're still working at another job, even while you're lying on the beach, enjoying a vacation.

And, best of all, your privacy is fully protected. To ensure complete confidentiality and maintain **your** control over your job search, **JOB BANK USA** will contact you personally and obtain your permission before releasing your resume to a prospective employer.

All you have to do to put this powerful capability to work for you is enroll in the **JOB BANK USA** data base. This data base holds the career records of people in virtually every occupational field and profession and at all management and skill levels. Consequently, organizations use the data base to recruit employees for the full range of their open jobs.

JOB BANK USA's clients range from some of the world's largest corporations to leading regional and local firms. They turn to **JOB BANK USA** to fill some of their best and most important jobs. These positions are seldom advertised in newspapers and are often filled exclusively from those individuals who are enrolled in the **JOB BANK USA** data base.

Through the power of Electronic Networking, every word in every record in the **JOB BANK USA** data base is read for every one of these employment opportunities. So, when you enroll in the **JOB BANK USA** Career Advancement Service, you get two important advantages: Your employment credentials will be seen and evaluated by those organizations which are actually hiring, all over the USA. And, you'll be competing for outstanding positions, which most people won't even know are available.

The JOB BANK USA Career Advancement Service is not a guarantee of a job. It does, however, put the power of Electronic Networking to work for you. And **that** gives you a genuine competitive advantage in today's tough job market.

Career Tool Kit

The old techniques for finding a job and advancing your career simply don't work any more. Instead, you need a set of powerful, new resources designed specifically for today's super-charged job market.

The **JOB BANK USA** Career Tool Kit is just such a resource! It has been developed to provide you with the most up-to-date resources, information and skills for managing your career successfully in the 1990's. The Career Tool Kit includes a quarterly job market newsletter; a private catalog of the very best career management books, services and software; the **JOB BANK USA** Career Fitness Program with its innovative techniques for building a healthy career; and toll free access to the **JOB BANK USA** staff for personal, private status reports and feedback on your job search.

All-in-all, the **JOB BANK USA** Career Advancement Service gives you a superb set of powerful, employment resources for the 1990's:

ELECTRONIC NETWORKING

- Conversion of your employment credentials into a personalized **JOB BANK USA** electronic career record;

- Storage and maintenance of your electronic career record in the **JOB BANK USA** data base for a full year;

- A toll free telephone number for updates and changes to your electronic career record anytime during the year;

- Unlimited referrals to **JOB BANK USA** clients with employment opportunities for which you are qualified;

- The absolute guarantee that **JOB BANK USA** will call you for approval *prior* to releasing your resume to a prospective employer;

CAREER TOOL KIT

- Quarterly issues of *CareerPLUS*, **JOB BANK USA**'s authoritative newsletter about the job market and the latest job search techniques;

- *The Career Fitness Catalog*, with special discounts on publications, services and other resources for effective career management;

- Access to **JOB BANK USA**'s exclusive *Career Fitness* program to help you find, win and keep the job you want in the 1990's; and

- A toll free telephone number for status reports and feedback on your job search.

All you have to do to enroll in the **JOB BANK USA** Career Advancement Service is complete the Data Base Enrollment Form on the next page. So, don't delay! Give your career the **JOB BANK USA** advantage! Enroll right away!

ENROLLMENT INSTRUCTIONS

Return your completed Data Base Enrollment Form, a copy of your current resume, your Discount Coupon and a check or money order for your $125.00 ($115.00 if including discount coupon) enrollment fee to:

JOB BANK USA--Enrollments
1420 Spring Hill Road
Suite 480
McLean, Virginia 22102

Please allow 10-14 days for processing.

JOB BANK USA, Incorporated
Data Base Enrollment Form

Please TYPE or PRINT all responses.

General Enrollment Information

Last Name	First Name	MI

Current Address	Apt. #	City	State	Zip

Home Phone	Business Phone	Relay Service Number
( )	( )	( )

Best time to be reached by phone?	Date available for work
Current/most recent salary	Minimum acceptable salary

What percentage of work-related travel is acceptable?   [ ] More than 50%   [ ] 10%-50%   [ ] Less than 10%

Where will you relocate?	[ ] Will NOT relocate	[ ] Anywhere in USA	[ ] Overseas
[ ] Northeast	[ ] Mid-Atlantic	[ ] Southeast	[ ] Midwest
[ ] Southwest	[ ] Mountain	[ ] West	[ ] Pacific Northwest
[ ] Only to the following States: _____			

Licenses/Certifications And Other Special Skills

License(s)/Certificate(s)	Number	Date
Security Clearance(s)	Level	Expiration

Language(s)/Proficiency

Computer Hardware/Software Applications

Signature

I hereby permit JOB BANK USA to submit the information I have entered on this form, and contained in my resume, to prospective employers. I affirm that the information I have provided herein is, to the best of my knowledge, true, complete and accurate. I also agree that this information may be retained in the JOB BANK USA data base, unless I request its deletion in writing. I understand that participation in JOB BANK USA is not a guarantee of employment. I also understand that JOB BANK USA disclaims any responsibility for any illegal use of the information provided in this form or accompanying resume by any prospective employer. JOB BANK USA is an Equal Employment Opportunity company.

Signature: _____   Date: _____

Payment Method

[ ] **Career Advancement Service @ $125.00**	*Thanks for enrolling in JOB BANK USA!*

[ ]   **Check or Money Order** (*payable to JOB BANK USA*)   [ ]   **Credit Card** (*see below*)

Card Type:	[ ] VISA [ ] MasterCard [ ] American Express
Card #:	|_|_|_|_|-|_|_|_|_|-|_|_|_|_|-|_|_|_|_| Expiration: |_|_|-|_|_|

Signature: _____   Date: _____

JOB BANK USA, Incorporated
Data Base Enrollment Form

Please TYPE or PRINT all responses.

General Enrollment Information

Last Name	First Name	MI

Current Address	Apt. #	City	State	Zip

Home Phone	Business Phone	Relay Service Number
( )	( )	( )

Best time to be reached by phone?	Date available for work
Current/most recent salary	Minimum acceptable salary

What percentage of work-related travel is acceptable?　[ ] More than 50%　[ ] 10%-50%　[ ] Less than 10%

Where will you relocate?	[ ] Will NOT relocate	[ ] Anywhere in USA	[ ] Overseas
[ ] Northeast	[ ] Mid-Atlantic	[ ] Southeast	[ ] Midwest
[ ] Southwest	[ ] Mountain	[ ] West	[ ] Pacific Northwest
[ ] Only to the following States: _____			

Licenses/Certifications And Other Special Skills

License(s)/Certificate(s)	Number	Date
Security Clearance(s)	Level	Expiration

Language(s)/Proficiency

Computer Hardware/Software Applications

Signature

I hereby permit JOB BANK USA to submit the information I have entered on this form, and contained in my resume, to prospective employers. I affirm that the information I have provided herein is, to the best of my knowledge, true, complete and accurate. I also agree that this information may be retained in the JOB BANK USA data base, unless I request its deletion in writing. I understand that participation in JOB BANK USA is not a guarantee of employment. I also understand that JOB BANK USA disclaims any responsibility for any illegal use of the information provided in this form or accompanying resume by any prospective employer. JOB BANK USA is an Equal Employment Opportunity company.

Signature: _____   Date: _____

Payment Method

[ ] **Career Advancement Service @ $125.00**	*Thanks for enrolling in JOB BANK USA!*

[ ] **Check or Money Order** (*payable to JOB BANK USA*)　　　[ ] **Credit Card** (*see below*)

Card Type:	[ ] VISA　　[ ] MasterCard　　[ ] American Express	
Card #:	|_|_|_|_|_|-|_|_|_|_|_|-|_|_|_|_|_|-|_|_|_|_|	Expiration: |_|_|-|_|_|

Signature: _____   Date: _____

JOB BANK USA, Incorporated
Data Base Enrollment Form

Please TYPE or PRINT all responses.

General Enrollment Information

Last Name	First Name	MI

Current Address	Apt. #	City	State	Zip

Home Phone	Business Phone	Relay Service Number
( )	( )	( )

Best time to be reached by phone?	Date available for work
Current/most recent salary	Minimum acceptable salary

What percentage of work-related travel is acceptable?   [ ] More than 50%   [ ] 10%-50%   [ ] Less than 10%

Where will you relocate?	[ ] Will NOT relocate	[ ] Anywhere in USA	[ ] Overseas
[ ] Northeast	[ ] Mid-Atlantic	[ ] Southeast	[ ] Midwest
[ ] Southwest	[ ] Mountain	[ ] West	[ ] Pacific Northwest

[ ] Only to the following States: ___ ___ ___ ___ ___ ___ ___ ___

Licenses/Certifications And Other Special Skills

License(s)/Certificate(s)	Number	Date
Security Clearance(s)	Level	Expiration

Language(s)/Proficiency

Computer Hardware/Software Applications

Signature

I hereby permit JOB BANK USA to submit the information I have entered on this form, and contained in my resume, to prospective employers. I affirm that the information I have provided herein is, to the best of my knowledge, true, complete and accurate. I also agree that this information may be retained in the JOB BANK USA data base, unless I request its deletion in writing. I understand that participation in JOB BANK USA is not a guarantee of employment. I also understand that JOB BANK USA disclaims any responsibility for any illegal use of the information provided in this form or accompanying resume by any prospective employer. JOB BANK USA is an Equal Employment Opportunity company.

Signature: _____   Date: _____

Payment Method

[ ] **Career Advancement Service @ $125.00**   *Thanks for enrolling in JOB BANK USA!*

[ ] **Check or Money Order** (*payable to JOB BANK USA*)   [ ] **Credit Card** (*see below*)

Card Type:	[ ] VISA [ ] MasterCard [ ] American Express
Card #:	|__|__|__|__|-|__|__|__|__|-|__|__|__|__|-|__|__|__|__| Expiration: |__|__|-|__|__|

Signature: _____   Date: _____

INDEX

153

CAREER RESOURCES

Contact Impact Publications to receive a free copy of their latest comprehensive and annotated catalog of career resources (books, subscriptions, training programs, videos, audiocassettes, computer software, and CD-ROM).

The following career resources are available directly from Impact Publications. Complete the following form or list the titles, include postage (see formula at the end), enclose payment, and send your order to:

IMPACT PUBLICATIONS
9104-N Manassas Drive
Manassas Park, VA 22111-5211
Tel. 703/361-7300 or Fax 703/335-9486

Orders from individuals must be prepaid by check, moneyorder, Visa or MasterCard number. We accept telephone and fax orders with a Visa or MasterCard number.

Qty.	TITLES	Price	TOTAL
RESUMES			
__	101 Resumes for Sure-Hire Results	$10.95	_____
__	Adams Resume Almanac	$10.95	_____
__	Best Resumes for $75,000+ Executive Jobs	$14.95	_____
__	Better Resumes for Executives and Professionals	$11.95	_____

__ Damn Good Resume Guide	$6.95	_____
__ Does Your Resume Wear Blue Jeans?	$7.95	_____
__ Does Your Resume Wear Combat Boots?	$7.95	_____
__ Dynamite Resumes	$10.95	_____
__ Electronic Resume Revolution	$12.95	_____
__ Electronic Resumes for the New Job Market	$11.95	_____
__ Encyclopedia of Job-Winning Resumes	$16.95	_____
__ High Impact Resumes and Letters	$14.95	_____
__ How to Prepare Your Curriculum Vitae	$14.95	_____
__ How to Write a Winning Resume	$8.95	_____
__ Just Resumes	$9.95	_____
__ No-Pain Resume Book	$14.95	_____
__ Overnight Resume	$7.95	_____
__ Perfect Resume	$12.00	_____
__ Perfect Resume Strategies	$12.50	_____
__ Power Resumes	$12.95	_____
__ Resume Catalog	$15.95	_____
__ Resume Kit	$9.95	_____
__ Resume Pro	$24.95	_____
__ Resume Solution	$10.95	_____
__ Resume Writing	$9.95	_____
__ Resume Writing Made Easy	$10.95	_____
__ Resumes for Advertising Careers	$9.95	_____
__ Resumes for Banking and Financial Careers	$9.95	_____
__ Resumes for Business Management Careers	$9.95	_____
__ Resumes for College Students and Recent Graduates	$9.95	_____
__ Resumes for Communications Careers	$9.95	_____
__ Resumes for Education Careers	$9.95	_____
__ Resumes for the Healthcare Professional	$12.95	_____
__ Resumes for High School Graduates	$9.95	_____
__ Resumes for High Tech Careers	$9.95	_____
__ Resumes for Midcareer Job Changers	$9.95	_____
__ Resumes for People Who Hate to Write Resumes	$12.95	_____
__ Resumes for Re-Entry: A Woman's Handbook	$10.95	_____
__ Resumes for Sales and Marketing Careers	$9.95	_____
__ Resumes for Scientific and Technical Careers	$9.95	_____
__ Resumes That Knock 'Em Dead	$7.95	_____
__ Resumes, Resumes, Resumes	$8.95	_____
__ Revising Your Resume	$13.95	_____
__ Smart Woman's Guide to Resumes & Job Hunting	$9.95	_____
__ Sure-Hire Resumes	$14.95	_____
__ Your First Resume	$8.95	_____

RESUME SOFTWARE (specify disk size and system)

__ Creative Resume	$139.95	_____
__ Perfect Resume Kit (Individual Version)	$49.95	_____
__ Perfect Resume Kit (Counselor Version)	$259.95	_____
__ Perfect Resume Kit (Lab Pack Version)	$639.95	_____
__ Perfect Resume Kit (Network Version)	$999.95	_____
__ Right Resume Writer I, II, and III	$299.95	_____
__ ResumeMaker	$49.95	_____

RESUME VIDEOS

__ Does Your Resume Wear Blue Jeans Resume Writing Workshop	$99.95	_____

__ The Miracle Resume $99.95 _____
__ Video Resume Writer $102.95 _____

COVER LETTERS

__ 175 High-Impact Cover Letters $10.95 _____
__ 200 Letters for Job Hunters $17.95 _____
__ Cover Letters That Don't Forget $8.95 _____
__ Cover Letters That Knock 'Em Dead $7.95 _____
__ Cover Letters That Will Get You the Job You Want $12.95 _____
__ Dynamic Cover Letters $6.95 _____
__ Dynamite Cover Letters $11.95 _____
__ INSTANT™ Job Hunting Letters (IBM software) $49.95 _____
__ Job Search Letters That Get Results $12.95 _____
__ Perfect Cover Letter $9.95 _____
__ Sure-Hire Cover Letters $10.95 _____

INTERVIEWS, NETWORKING & SALARY NEGOTIATIONS

__ 60 Seconds and You're Hired! $9.95 _____
__ Dynamite Answers to Interview Questions $11.95 _____
__ Dynamite Salary Negotiation $12.95 _____
__ Great Connections $11.95 _____
__ How to Work a Room $9.95 _____
__ Interview for Success $11.95 _____
__ New Network Your Way to Job and Career Success $12.95 _____
__ The Secrets of Savvy Networking $11.99 _____
__ Sweaty Palms $9.95 _____

SKILLS, TESTING, SELF-ASSESSMENT, EMPOWERMENT

__ 7 Habits of Highly Effective People $11.00 _____
__ Discover the Best Jobs for You $11.95 _____
__ Do What You Are $14.95 _____
__ Do What You Love, the Money Will Follow $10.95 _____
__ Finding the Hat That Fits $10.00 _____
__ Stop Postponing the Rest of Your Life $9.95 _____
__ What Color Is Your Parachute? $14.95 _____
__ Where Do I Go From Here With My Life? $10.95 _____
__ Wishcraft $10.95 _____

DRESS, APPEARANCE, IMAGE

__ Dressing Smart in the 90's (women) $9.95 _____
__ John Molloy's New Dress for Success (men) $10.95 _____
__ Red Socks Don't Work! (men) $14.95 _____
__ The Winning Image $17.95 _____
__ Women's Dress for Success $9.95 _____

JOB SEARCH STRATEGIES AND TACTICS

__ 40+ Job Hunting Guide $23.95 _____
__ 110 Biggest Mistakes Job Hunters Make $14.95 _____
__ Career Fitness $19.95 _____
__ Change Your Job, Change Your Life $14.95 _____
__ Complete Job Finder's Guide to the 90s $13.95 _____

__ Complete Job Search Handbook	$12.95	_____
__ Cracking the Over-50 Job Market	$11.95	_____
__ Dynamite Tele-Search	$10.95	_____
__ Electronic Job Search Revolution	$12.95	_____
__ Five Secrets to Finding a Job	$12.95	_____
__ Guerrilla Tactics in the New Job Market	$5.99	_____
__ How to Get Interviews From Classified Job Ads	$14.95	_____
__ Job Hunting After 50	$12.95	_____
__ Joyce Lain Kennedy's Career Book	$29.95	_____
__ Knock 'Em Dead	$19.95	_____
__ Professional's Private Sector Job Finder	$18.95	_____
__ Right Place At the Right Time	$11.95	_____
__ Rites of Passage At $100,000+	$29.95	_____
__ Super Job Search	$22.95	_____
__ Who's Hiring Who	$9.95	_____
__ Work in the New Economy	$14.95	_____

BEST JOBS AND EMPLOYERS FOR THE 90s

__ 100 Best Companies to Work for in America	$27.95	_____
__ 100 Best Jobs for the 1990s and Beyond	$19.95	_____
__ 101 Careers	$12.95	_____
__ American Almanac of Jobs and Salaries	$17.00	_____
__ America's 50 Fastest Growing Jobs	$9.95	_____
__ America's Fastest Growing Employers	$14.95	_____
__ Best Jobs for the 1990s and Into the 21st Century	$12.95	_____
__ Hoover's Handbook of American Business (annual)	$34.95	_____
__ Hoover's Handbook of World Business (annual)	$32.95	_____
__ Job Seeker's Guide to 1000 Top Employers	$22.95	_____
__ Jobs! What They Are, Where They Are, What They Pay	$13.95	_____
__ Jobs 1994	$15.95	_____
__ New Emerging Careers	$14.95	_____
__ Top Professions	$10.95	_____

KEY DIRECTORIES

__ American Salaries and Wages Survey	$94.95	_____
__ Career Training Sourcebook	$24.95	_____
__ Careers Encyclopedia	$39.95	_____
__ Complete Guide for Occupational Exploration	$29.95	_____
__ Dictionary of Occupational Titles	$39.95	_____
__ Directory of Executive Recruiters (annual)	$39.95	_____
__ Directory of Outplacement Firms	$74.95	_____
__ Directory of Special Programs for Minority Group Members	$31.95	_____
__ Encyclopedia of Careers and Vocational Guidance	$129.95	_____
__ Enhanced Guide for Occupational Exploration	$29.95	_____
__ Government Directory of Addresses and Telephone Numbers	$99.95	_____
__ Hoover's Handbook of American Business	$34.95	_____
__ Internships (annual)	$29.95	_____
__ Job Bank Guide to Employment Services (annual)	$149.95	_____
__ Job Hunter's Sourcebook	$59.95	_____
__ Moving and Relocation Directory	$149.00	_____
__ National Directory of Addresses & Telephone Numbers	$129.95	_____
__ National Job Bank (annual)	$249.95	_____
__ National Trade and Professional Associations	$79.95	_____

__ Minority Organizations	$49.95	_____
__ Occupational Outlook Handbook	$22.95	_____
__ Personnel Executives Contactbook	$149.00	_____
__ Places Rated Almanac	$21.95	_____
__ Professional Careers Sourcebook	$79.95	_____

INTERNATIONAL, OVERSEAS, AND TRAVEL JOBS

__ Almanac of International Jobs and Careers	$19.95	_____
__ Complete Guide to International Jobs & Careers	$13.95	_____
__ Flying High in Travel	$16.95	_____
__ Guide to Careers in World Affairs	$14.95	_____
__ How to Get a Job in Europe	$17.95	_____
__ How to Get a Job in the Pacific Rim	$17.95	_____
__ Jobs for People Who Love Travel	$12.95	_____
__ Jobs in Paradise	$12.95	_____
__ Jobs in Russia and the Newly Independent States	$15.95	_____
__ Teaching English Abroad	$15.95	_____
__ Work Your Way Around the World	$17.95	_____

PUBLIC-ORIENTED CAREERS

__ Almanac of American Government Jobs and Careers	$19.95	_____
__ Complete Guide to Public Employment	$19.95	_____
__ Federal Jobs in Law Enforcement	$15.95	_____
__ Find a Federal Job Fast!	$12.95	_____
__ Government Job Finder	$16.95	_____
__ Jobs and Careers With Nonprofit Organizations	$14.95	_____
__ Non-Profit's Job Finder	$16.95	_____
__ The Right SF 171 Writer	$19.95	_____

COMPUTER SOFTWARE

__ JOBHUNT™ Quick and Easy Employer Contacts	$49.95	_____
__ INSTANT™ Job Hunting Letters	$49.95	_____
__ Ultimate Job Finder	$59.95	_____
__ You're Hired!	$49.95	_____

VIDEOS

__ Dialing for Jobs	$129.00	_____
__ Find the Job You Want...and Get It! (4 videos)	$229.95	_____
__ How to Present a Professional Image (2 videos)	$149.95	_____
__ Inside Secrets of Interviewing	$39.95	_____
__ Insider's Guide to Competitive Interviewing	$59.95	_____
__ Networking Your Way to Success	$89.95	_____
__ Very Quick Job Search	$129.00	_____
__ Winning at Job Hunting in the 90s	$89.95	_____

JOB LISTINGS & VACANCY ANNOUNCEMENTS

__ Community (Nonprofit) Jobs (1 year)	$69.00	_____
__ Federal Career Opportunities (6 biweekly issues)	$39.00	_____
__ International Employment Gazette (6 biweekly issues)	$35.00	_____
__ The Search Bulletin (6 issues)	$97.00	_____

MILITARY

__ America's Top Military Careers	$19.95	_____
__ Beyond the Uniform	$12.95	_____
__ Civilian Career Guide	$12.95	_____
__ Does Your Resume Wear Combat Boots?	$7.95	_____
__ From Army Green to Corporate Gray	$15.95	_____
__ From Navy Blue to Corporate Gray	$17.95	_____
__ Job Search: Marketing Your Military Experience	$14.95	_____
__ Re-Entry	$13.95	_____
__ Retiring From the Military	$22.95	_____

WOMEN AND SPOUSES

__ Balancing Career and Family	$7.95	_____
__ Congratulations: You've Been Fired!	$8.95	_____
__ Doing It All Isn't Everything	$19.95	_____
__ Female Advantage	$19.95	_____
__ New Relocating Spouse's Guide to Employment	$14.95	_____
__ Resumes for Re-Entry: A Handbook for Women	$10.95	_____
__ Smart Woman's Guide to Resumes and Job Hunting	$9.95	_____
__ Survival Guide for Women	$16.95	_____
__ Women's Job Search Handbook	$12.95	_____

MINORITIES AND DISABLED

__ Best Companies for Minorities	$12.00	_____
__ Directory of Special Programs for Minority Group Members	$31.95	_____
__ Job Strategies for People With Disabilities	$14.95	_____
__ Minority Organizations	$49.95	_____
__ Work, Sister, Work	$19.95	_____

COLLEGE STUDENTS

__ 150 Best Companies for Liberal Arts Grads	$12.95	_____
__ Career Planning and Development for College Students and Recent Graduates	$17.95	_____
__ Careers for College Majors	$29.95	_____
__ College Majors and Careers	$15.95	_____
__ Complete Resume and Job Search Book for College Students	$9.95	_____
__ Graduating to the 9-5 World	$11.95	_____
__ How You Really Get Hired	$11.00	_____
__ Kiplinger's Career Starter	$10.95	_____
__ Liberal Arts Jobs	$10.95	_____

ENTREPRENEURSHIP AND SELF-EMPLOYMENT

__ 101 Best Businesses to Start	$15.00	_____
__ 184 Businesses Anyone Can Start	$12.95	_____
__ Best Home-Based Businesses for the 90s	$10.95	_____
__ Entrepreneur's Guide to Starting a Successful Business	$16.95	_____
__ Have You Got What It Takes?	$12.95	_____
__ How to Start, Run, and Stay in Business	$12.95	_____
__ Kiplinger's Working for Yourself	$13.95	_____

__ Mid-Career Entrepreneur $17.95 _____
__ When Friday Isn't Payday $12.99 _____

CD-ROM

__ America's Top Jobs $295.00 _____
__ Encyclopedia of Associations $995.00 _____
__ Encyclopedia of Careers and Vocational Guidance $199.95 _____
__ Job-Power Source (Individual Version) $49.95 _____
__ Job-Power Source (Professional Version) $149.95 _____
__ Occupational Outlook CD-ROM $29.95 _____

SUBTOTAL   _____

Virginia residents add 4½% sales tax   _____

POSTAGE/HANDLING ($4.00 for first
    title and $1.00 for each additional book) $4.00

Number of additional titles x $1.00 ----------   _____

TOTAL ENCLOSED ------------------------   _____

SHIP TO:

NAME _____

ADDRESS _____

_____

_____

[ ] I enclose check/moneyorder for $ _____ made
    payable to IMPACT PUBLICATIONS.

[ ] Please charge $ _____ to my credit card:

Card # _____

Expiration date: _____/_____

Signature _____

We accept official purchase orders from libraries, educational institutions,
and government offices.